Minding
the Kids

Minding
the Kids

A PRACTICAL GUIDE TO
EMPLOYING NANNIES, CARE GIVERS,
BABY SITTERS, AND AU PAIRS

Ruth S. Elliott
with Jim Savage

PRENTICE HALL PRESS
New York • London • Toronto • Sydney • Tokyo

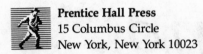

Prentice Hall Press
15 Columbus Circle
New York, New York 10023

PRENTICE HALL PRESS and colophon are registered
trademarks of Simon & Schuster, Inc.

Library of Congress Cataloging-in-Publication Data

Elliott, Ruth S.
Minding the kids: a practical guide to employing nannies, care givers,
baby sitters and au pairs / Ruth S. Elliott with Jim Savage.
    p. cm.
  Includes index.
  ISBN 0-13-690728-8 (v. 1)
    1. Childcare services—United States. 2. Au pairs—United
States. 3. Baby sitters—United States. 4. Nannies—United States.
I. Savage, Jim. II. Title.
HQ778.7.U6E45   1990   89-30445
                                                            CIP

Designed by Irving Perkins Associates

Manufactured in the United States

10 9 8 7 6 5 4 3 2 1

First Edition

Acknowledgments

We'd like to thank

Nancy Trichter, for agreeing that there was a need for a book on this subject and for ultimately ensuring that this particular book be published.

Allen E. Kaye, New York City immigration attorney and past president of the American Immigration Lawyers' Association, for editing information relating to the employment of foreign workers.

Lester Wohl, Konigsberg, Wolf and Co., certified public accountant, for sharing his knowledge of laws relating to monetary and tax issues.

Jeffrey M. Elliott, managing partner, Hartman & Craven, attorneys-at-law, for researching legal questions.

Gail Winston, our editor, who believed in the manuscript, took it, and ran with it.

All the parents, care givers, and children from across the United States who shared their experiences with us.

All the many professionals—educators, doctors, psychiatrists, psychologists, social workers, and counselors—who so generously shared their knowledge and expertise.

Monica Hughes and Liz Rizzi, who always said "no problem."

Contents

Why We Wrote This Book

For most of our parents' generation, the answer to childcare was simple: Primary care was provided by a mother who stayed at home with the kids while dad was off at work. Now, more often than not, both parents have jobs—that is, when there are two parents. Family life in America has changed, and the childcare choices we are faced with are new and challenging ones.

We have no guidelines to work with, no historical precedents to let us know that the decisions we make are the best ones for our children. Many of us have little more to go on than our own good intentions. Yet, like parents of every generation, we need to know that when we're not around, our children are in responsible hands: safe, secure, and cared for with love and understanding.

Unfortunately, it's not a foregone conclusion. We no longer live in a society where an extended family—grandparents, cousins, uncles, and aunts—helps take care of the children. Most of us now have to look outside the family for childcare.

That was the situation we both faced when our own children were born. Although each of us wanted our kids to have the best possible care, we knew that we and our spouses couldn't be there all the time to ensure that they got the kind of warm, reliable care they needed.

We had the advice of friends, of course (some good, some bad). We had the advice of our own parents (some relevant, some useless). And when we looked at our alternatives—daycare centers, group care in someone else's home, individual in-home childcare— we both decided that if our children had to be cared for by someone else, we wanted them to have the security of one-to-one relationships with loving, responsible people in their own homes. And when we felt a strong need for a guide to help us make these important decisions about our children's care, there simply wasn't one.

We met each other pushing carriages. As our children grew and our social world included more and more parents of young children, we realized that we weren't alone in our predicament. Just about everyone we knew expressed the same feelings about childcare we had—that they were being forced to make important decisions about in-home care through trial and error.

We began to feel that it wasn't just the parents in our neighborhood who felt that way. Soon, through a network of friends and acquaintances, we started speaking with other parents across the country. When many of them told us of their experiences and expressed the same need that we had for a guide, we decided to research the matter further.

The statistical evidence gleaned while doing our preliminary work substantiated our intuition (and our early conversations with other parents) that a vast number of parents were looking for in-home childcare solutions. Census Bureau statistics show that more than half the mothers of children under six are employed outside the home, that by 1990 husband-wife households with only one working spouse will represent only 14 percent of all households (compared to 43 percent in 1960), and that today approximately one-third of working mothers arrange for childcare in their own homes.

Our research deepened our understanding of the numerous issues involved in in-home childcare and enabled us to move beyond our own intuition and limited experience to create a book with a much wider application. We sent hundreds of questionnaires to parents throughout the country, and a great many responded with thoughtful, honest replies about their childcare needs, expectations, and experiences. We also prepared a questionnaire for care givers, and their responses helped us understand the employees' side of the childcare equation. We spoke face to face with parents, children, and care givers, and many of them opened up their hearts to us about their experiences and emotions. In addition, we spoke with numerous professionals in childcare and related fields—educators, child psychiatrists and psychologists, pediatricians, and others—who shared their knowledge and expertise with us. Now we'd like to share what we've learned with you.

This book is about finding and growing with the people who will take care of your children in the most secure of all environments, your own home. It's a book about options, about not limiting yourself (and your child) before you've even begun, about finding solutions you'll be happy with—and that you'll be able to afford.

We hope this book will be your guide, and that it will help put your mind at rest.

CHAPTER 1

Your Child Is on the Way

You're about to become parents . . . what do you do now? Love your baby, that's a given. Worry—that's a given too. But what about when you get the precious bundle home? When you go back to work? When you just need a break?

You probably have a lot of friends who are more than ready to give you advice. Maybe not just friends, either. Mothers, mothers-in-law, strangers on the street—they all see a big belly and can't wait to tell you what to do. And some of their advice makes sense.

But how do you tell the gold from the dross? As family therapist and Fordham University parent educator Dr. Sandra Rodman Mann suggests, "Look at the source of the advice—friends want to be helpful, of course, but they have underlying issues of their own."

When it comes to childcare, the best advice, and the only advice that works every time, is: You have choices, every step of the way, and you have to choose which one is best for you and your family.

VISIONS OF LIFE WITH BABY

What are your visions of life with baby? Perhaps you secretly believe that your child will be the one that's perfect, the one that sleeps through the night, the one everybody loves without reservation. But the facts are that only you, and perhaps some other family members, will love your child heart and soul, that no baby sleeps through the night right away, and that nobody's perfect.

Or perhaps you feel that the responsibility of taking care of a child is too overwhelming, that it's more than you can handle. You can't imagine going back to work and leaving your baby behind, yet on the other hand you can't imagine being left alone with a helpless newborn day after day. The idea (and the reality) of having a baby fills you with terror.

Take heart. Most people, despite the stress, do cope. And you will too.

Like all parents, you have expectations, hopes, and dreams for your children. And even though you may deny it, you probably feel anxiety, stress, and fear as well. Nobody knows ahead of time what life with baby will really be like.

WHAT TO EXPECT

The first few months of your baby's life will be a period filled with unforeseen events. You may change your mind about when and if you're going back to work, you may find your finances strained to the limit, you may have problems in your marriage, and you will probably feel more exhausted than you've ever felt in your life. You will also be adapting to the life and personality of a unique new person.

This is a difficult time. According to Dr. Mann, "no decision you make [at this time] is without ambivalence." And Fretta Reitzes, director of the Parenting Center at New York City's 92nd Street Y, says many new parents feel "overwhelmed."

Faced with all the stress that goes along with new parenthood, it's no wonder many people lose confidence in their own judgment and become willing to defer to others in making important decisions about childcare. The best suggestion we can make about this tendency is don't give in to it!

Only you really know what's best for your family. Accepting this responsibility, then closing out the world and taking stock of what exists in reality, is one of the hardest—and most rewarding—things about being a parent.

If you're married, you don't have to do it alone. In fact, discussing your real childcare needs and trying to determine your real options may even strengthen the ties of your marriage as it helps you build the confidence you need to become an effective parenting team.

YOUR REAL CHILDCARE NEEDS

In planning for childcare, the quickest and easiest way to rid yourself of illusions is to sit down and figure out what you expect your real needs to be. You probably don't know for sure. You're still feeling your way now, and it is only through the experience of being with and loving your child that you will get to know what kind of care he or she needs in reality. But never mind that your answers aren't perfect at first. You can always change your mind later.

Every baby is different. There are some needs that all children share, and primary among them (along with food and shelter) is the need to be nurtured, cared for, and loved. Your child—whether active or quiet, content or colicky—will not be an exception. Here are some of the questions that are pertinent to your early childcare decisions.

When you get home from the hospital, will you need help from someone outside your immediate family?

Perhaps one of the new grandmothers is coming in from out of town to stay with you for the first couple of weeks. You realize she'll try to take over your household, run everything her way, and drive you both crazy . . . but she'll also cook your meals, shop, and help you bathe and dress the baby. The trade-off is worth it, and the extra hand will give you at least a little bit of needed rest during the first couple of weeks of your baby's life.

If a grandmother is not coming, do you feel that you can cope with a newborn's needs—from feeding six or eight times a day to changing diapers to sponge bathing and eye cleaning—and keep your house running at the same time? What if your baby gets a gas bubble at 4:00 A.M. and cries for an hour before going back to sleep—how will that affect your equilibrium?

Maybe you need a baby nurse, or someone to clean and cook for you, or perhaps you should hire a full-time, permanent care giver right away. Whatever your decision, it isn't made in a vacuum; it's actually based on lots of other variables.

Is your baby going to be breast-fed?

Nursing is not as natural and easy as many of its proponents claim; although it can be very fulfilling for both mother and child, it often takes a lot of time, encouragement and energy to get started. A baby nurse who has worked with breast-feeding mothers might be your best bet.

Are mom and dad both planning to go back to work right away?

If you are, it may make sense to look for a permanent care giver immediately, perhaps even before your baby is born. That way you can get to know the person you will be leaving your child with during the short postnatal recovery period before you both start working again. You'll have the time to get used to her, to let her know what you want, and to become adjusted to the idea—and the reality—of being a family with two working parents.

If you're not both planning to go back to work immediately, you may want to take some time to get to know your baby, to be alone and deepen the bonds between yourself and your child. Or you may want to hire a temporary helper, someone who will give you a little rest until you and your baby have settled into a comfortable routine. You may be in a position where you can defer any decisions about permanent childcare.

It all sounds fine, simple, clear, and rational. But it doesn't always work out that way. No matter what your plans are now, the expectation and the eventual reality might not mesh when the baby actually comes home. You may find instead that, even though you planned to return to work right away, you're emotionally incapable of leaving your baby so soon; or that, despite your desire to stay home with your new arrival, your financial needs are far greater than expected and going back to work is the only way you can possibly make ends meet.

Going back to work is a difficult decision for virtually every mother and, although there is nothing inherently wrong with it, in many ways it adds a great deal of stress to the new parents' life. It's not just another demand to juggle; sometimes it seems as though this particular demand makes the whole thing almost too much to handle. Some children do have trouble adapting when their mothers go back to work. And on top of the baby's difficulty, along with your own fatigue and anxiety, there's an additional emotional strain—very often, mothers feel a strong sense of guilt from the moment they leave their child behind in someone else's hands.

Many working mothers have told us that the guilt is almost

inevitable, that it goes with the territory. But if you can deal with your situation on a rational level, it's something that can be, if not overcome, then at least mitigated by the reality of your situation.

If you are forced to work for financial reasons, it's certainly much more than a rationalization to say that having someone else take care of your baby is the best thing for you and your baby—it's objective reality. If you do not bring in enough money on one salary to allow yourselves a minimal sense of security, then you can't give your baby all your love; your life will be too burdened with fear and financial worry . . . as well as anger at your child for putting you in such an untenable situation.

When a mother chooses to go back to work, and it's not based on actual financial need, it's important to understand both what will be lost and what will be gained from the decision.

On the negative side, you won't be a constant, active witness to your child's development from a totally helpless, passive being to a person who fully participates in the world. But on the positive side, if you feel that working will make you feel more fulfilled and happy, then it might also mean that you have more to give to your child . . . even if you have less time.

But if I choose to hire a permanent person, how do I know whom to hire?

Hiring a care giver is a very important and, at times, very complex decision. There is much to consider, from your actual day-to-day needs to your subconscious motivations. If it's possible, don't rush into a decision. Think things through carefully, and try to give yourselves the time you need to feel as comfortable as possible with the choices you're making.

Fretta Reitzes says, "Parents who are hiring for the first time often do not understand the special nature of the relationship." Childcare is *not* just another job. It's a job that requires love (for your child) and entails a level of intimacy (with your entire family) that very few other jobs demand.

Ms. Reitzes stresses the absolute necessity for parents to talk with each other about their real childcare needs, and to make their decisions based on a thorough assessment.

Dr. Sandra Rodman Mann agrees that parents should try to focus as specifically as possible on what they want before hiring. And she cautions parents who are not yet familiar with their new family needs and may hire the wrong person for the wrong reasons, "Very often we hire people who hook into something in us. They remind you of your mother, they threaten you, you feel they will take control and relieve you of responsibility." But your child is your responsibility, and in the end you have to decide who's in charge. If you give up control now it's very hard to take back the reigns later.

How much can you afford for childcare?

Your answer to this question determines what type of care giver you can even consider hiring. In general, childcare in your own home *is* more expensive than some of the other available options, but day-care centers and group home care cost money too, and finding reliable and nurturing group care often feels like finding a friend in a city of strangers.

If you have no financial worries, you can afford an experienced, trained nanny; if you have very little extra money to spend on childcare, you may consider an au pair who will take care of your child in return for room and board. If you really want and need in-home childcare, you can generally figure out a creative way to pay for it.

There are times when hiring someone to care for your children in your own home is not only more convenient and reassuring than taking them to a center, but a relative bargain as well. For example, if you have more than one child (even if one goes to school and only needs after-school care), it often makes good economic sense for families of limited means to go with an in-home solution. As one Oregon father said, "In-home childcare is easier with three small children, and it's not more expensive."

Are you prepared to have someone involved in your household and with members of your family?

Some people feel very private about their personal space and their family relationships. As one San Francisco mother who hired live-in childcare help remarked, "It's so trying living with someone who's not related to you. You don't have privacy . . . in some ways it's harder to adjust to this than to having kids."

IS IN-HOME CHILDCARE RIGHT FOR YOU?
A CHECKLIST

Pro

[ ] Is it important to you that your child have a one-to-one relationship with his or her care giver?

[ ] Do you want to have total control over how your child is cared for?

[ ] Do you want to know your child is cared for at home when he or she is sick?

[ ] Will you feel more comfortable if your child is in a familiar setting?

Con

or [ ] Is it important that your child be cared for in a social setting?

or [ ] Are you happier getting input on childcare decisions from professionals?

or [ ] Is the care giver's health and attendance a greater concern so that you're more comfortable with a center's built-in backup?

or [ ] Do you want your child to discover new environments, and learn to thrive in a variety of places?

[　] Is the convenience of having someone come to you important? *or* [　] Are you flexible enough to take your child somewhere in the morning, and pick him or her up in the afternoon?

[　] Do you need to arrange special hours for your child's care? *or* [　] Are you comfortable with always arriving at a set time to drop off or pick up your child?

[　] Is in-home care within your family's financial capabilities? *or* [　] Will a daycare center, group or subsidized care create less strain on your resources?

There are literally hundreds of questions to consider when making childcare decisions, and sometimes it seems as though each answer leads to a dozen new questions. Should we hire in-home care, or should we opt for a daycare center, family care, or a neighbor's play group? If we decide we want someone in our home, should it be a baby nurse, a housekeeper, a full-time or part-time care giver, live-in help, or an au pair, or should we hire nobody at all? The options are there, and some would call them daunting. But approached with thought, caution, and a clear sense of what you need, they will no longer seem so overwhelming. And even if there is no one right solution for you—or for anyone else—it's okay. There are many options that work.

Perhaps the most important thing to remember when you make a decision about who will take care of your child—now or at any time in the future—is that you can change your mind if it's not working out. You're never locked in.

CHAPTER 2

Baby Nurses and Other Newborn Options

Imagine . . . you're just home from the hospital. You feel:

- Exhausted

- Exhilarated

- Depressed

- Amazed

- All of the above and much, much more

If your responses run the gamut from utter joy to total panic, you're completely normal. And if the diaper doesn't stay on, or you don't find the right bottle temperature, or the baby seems too fragile, or you simply don't know what to do—that's normal too. You may need help.

You can call your pediatrician; he or she will most likely be helpful and supportive. But your doctor won't be there to hold your hand, or to soothe your baby when you feel like you can't go on. You might call one of your new baby's grandmothers; after all, they do have some experience bringing up children, but they might want to take over, and you want to maintain control over the decisions regarding your child's life. Your friends, too, may offer help, but in all likelihood they can't be there with you night and day; they have their own lives to live. You might find that the best answer is a baby nurse.

WHAT KIND OF HELP DO YOU NEED— BABY NURSE OR HOUSEKEEPER?

The only thing about this question the parents and professionals we interviewed agreed on was to disagree—passionately. Here are their views.

Dr. Judy Goldstein, associate director of pediatrics at New York's Lenox Hill Hospital and the mother of two young children, told us, "Moms should have baby nurses. They make life easier and teach the mother. Nurses are trained, informed pros who only stay ten to fourteen days; they lend a tired mother a helping hand. And many new moms are fraught with anxiety; the baby nurse relieves some anxiety about the mothering aspects. The emotional mileage you get out of a baby nurse is well worth it."

Another prominent pediatrician, Dr. William Robins Brown, Jr., had a different opinion. "Mothers are better served by having housekeepers than baby nurses. Baby nurses just delay the process of taking care of your own child for a week or two. Mothers need help with housework, not with the childcare."

Dr. Goldstein disagreed, "Some mothers are more anxious if they suddenly have to supervise a housekeeper; for this it's better to rely on your usual support system of husband and friends for traditional housekeeping than to hire someone new."

And obstetrician Carol Livoti declared unequivocally, "Baby nurses are not a luxury; they're a necessity." She added, "Since delivery is often quite arduous, mothers need a break, particularly if the mother has had a Caesarean section." Among Dr. Livoti's patients, although some feel a baby nurse is an intrusion, most women have made their baby nurse arrangements long before delivery (often finding someone through the recommendation of a friend).

Charlene Stokamer, a childbirth educator and R.N., said, "I don't recommend a baby nurse. The mother needs a housekeeper or a mother-type who will mother the mother. Otherwise it's like starting from scratch after the baby nurse leaves. Baby nurses are often not nurses; they might have some training or even no training at all and many don't know anything about breast-feeding."

On the other hand, many baby nurses do have training and years of experience, and their presence can be a godsend to the exhausted new mother who hasn't the faintest idea how to cope with a newborn and the sudden changes in her home.

As for the real-life experiences of parents, a Staten Island mother told us, "I had a baby nurse and I cried when she left. I was terrified to be left with a newborn."

A mother in Los Angeles described what happened to her as "dreadful," saying the baby nurse "came in and tried to take over, telling us what to do with no concern for our feelings. And she didn't know anything besides."

This wide disparity is reflected in the experiences of the authors: While Ruth's baby nurse had a certificate showing her training and had taken care of thirty-five babies (with references checked), Ruth didn't ask her about her knowledge or feelings about breast-feeding—and indeed she knew nothing about it. Fortunately, with the aid of a book on breast-feeding, Ruth managed. On the other hand, Jim's wife had a baby nurse who helped her get started nursing, who encouraged both parents and left them with a feeling of confidence in their own ability to take care of their baby.

ANOTHER ALTERNATIVE FOR
FAMILIES WITH NEWBORNS

Several agencies around the country specialize in postpartum home care—care designed to aid the mother—not just the baby or the household. Promoted as part-time practical and emotional help for mothers, "postpartum" agencies provide workers who cook, clean, and do errands for families with newborns. How do they differ from housekeepers? Because postpartum agency employees have some knowledge of neonatal care (from childbirth classes or La Leche League courses), they claim to be particularly sensitive to the needs of mothers with newborns.

Before you can evaluate what your own family's postpartum childcare and/or housekeeping needs will be, it's important for you to know what a baby nurse actually does.

WHAT DOES A BABY NURSE DO?

A good baby nurse is sympathetic to your wants and needs and, perhaps most important, has seen it all before. Claire Luppi, vice-president of New York's Avalon Agency (one of the largest baby nurse agencies in the country), says the baby nurse takes care of the baby, gives the mother a rest, and teaches parents the basics of baby care. Baby nurse Vivienne Brown says she shows parents how to bathe, feed, and handle the baby; how to relieve gas and discomfort; how to clean the umbilical cord; and other very basic matters of practical infant care.

How basic can these matters get? Vivienne once walked through the door of a new client's home to find this sad scene: a mother and baby crying, and a new father on the edge of total frustration. It seems the father had prepared and warmed a bottle of formula; the baby had been sucking for quite some time but she still seemed hungry. Vivienne noticed what the parents had not—the father had neglected to remove the disk from the nipple ring, thus blocking the flow of milk.

A baby nurse will help set up the nursery; if asked, she may come and prepare for the baby's arrival while mother and child are still in the hospital. And she will handle virtually anything that directly concerns the baby, including changing dirty diapers, making up the crib, and washing the baby bottles. She's not there to clean your house or cook your meals or do your shopping. She may do light errands, scramble up a couple of eggs or sweep—but unless you make it clear from the start that those are among her duties (and she accepts them), don't count on it.

Some nurses also practice a little personal psychology on new parents. The first thing Katie Law of Los Angeles does is send the mother to bed; her take-charge attitude reflects her background as an assistant to a nanny in the British royal family, and she says her clients find it comforting.

Ermine Crawford of Brooklyn believes in the power of positive thinking; she recognizes that "some new moms are very flexible and some are very dependent and nervous." She tells all new moms that they can do whatever it is they try to do. As for fathers, Ermine says, "some think they are going to break the baby because the baby is so small." She tells them, "Daddy, you're going to change the diaper." Even if it ends up lopsided, she applauds their efforts. And she takes obvious pride in the fact that by the time she leaves, fathers as well as mothers have learned the basics.

Dr. Carol Livoti agrees that the baby nurse can be a strong confidence builder. She also told us, "Baby nurses I know get the baby up and changed in the middle of the night, tiptoe into the mother's bedroom and put the baby right in position for feeding. After feeding they take the baby away for burping and changing the diaper." Of course that describes an ideal baby nurse . . . but there are many who are far from ideal.

A TYPICAL DAY IN THE LIFE OF A BABY NURSE

Although every baby, every family, and every baby nurse is different, here's a close approximation of what a typical day in the life of a baby nurse might look like.

Let's assume the baby is five days old. At three days, the mother and child came home from the hospital; the baby nurse, having already prepared the nursery, was awaiting their arrival. Now, two days later, everything is settling down.

5:00 A.M. The baby wakes up hungry. The baby nurse, who is asleep on a cot in the nursery, wakes up too. She picks up the baby, discovers that he's soaked through his clothes and bedding, quickly changes his diaper and clothes and brings him into the mother for a feeding. Because she's a nursing mother, no bottle need be prepared. But the baby nurse is there to place warm compresses on the mother's breasts if they've become engorged, in order to help the milk start flowing. Once the nursing starts going smoothly, the baby nurse goes back into the nursery and changes the baby's bedding. By this time the infant is finished nursing on one breast, and the baby nurse returns to burp him and, if necessary, change his diaper. She then brings the baby back to feed on the second breast. After nursing is finished, everyone goes back to bed.

8:00 A.M. Same routine, but this time the baby nurse stays up, showers, dresses, and makes breakfast for herself and the mother. She also sterilizes bottles and, if necessary, prepares formula.

12:00 P.M. The cycle of changing, feeding, burping, and feeding repeats. After lunch, the baby nurse and mother may take the baby out for a walk.

3:30 P.M.   Same thing, but this time the baby doesn't go back to sleep. He has a gas bubble and cries. He is apparently inconsolable, but the nurse massages his back, walks him around, and burps him until he is finally calm. The nurse then takes a short break while the mother and father (who has worked a short day) look after the baby.

7:00 P.M.   Another feeding, another change. The nurse encourages the father (who is still a little tentative) to hold and burp the baby; she then helps him change a diaper. After baby's back to sleep, it's time for the nurse's dinner.

10:30 P.M.   Process repeats, followed by a sponge bath for the baby, with parents in attendance. Everyone goes to sleep.

2:00 A.M.   This time the baby doesn't go back to sleep after feeding. Nurse walks baby around, etc., finally getting back to bed at 4:00 A.M.

DIFFERENT FAMILIES, DIFFERENT NEEDS

It's important that you discuss and clarify your family's childcare needs at least two months before the baby is due. This will give you time to act on your decision without feeling impelled to accept a person or an arrangement that you're not happy with. If you just want someone to cook dinner and clean your house while you get to know your baby, then a baby nurse is not for you, and you would be better off with a housekeeper. If you want *some* support getting started with your baby, but you also require help around the house, postpartum nursing care might be for you. But even if you decide on a baby nurse, your wants and needs may differ from someone else's.

You have to decide whether you want a nurse who will sleep in, or one who will work eight-hour days. Do you want someone to simply relieve you when you're exhausted, or someone to provide total care? If you expect to have a Caesarean section (C-section) you will probably want someone who is willing to do more of the heavy physical work while you recuperate, and if you have older children, you may want someone who can relate to them as well as to the new baby.

Your needs are not only physical and practical, they are also emotional and philosophical. You could have a disaster on your hands if you hire someone whose ideas about handling newborns differ markedly from your own. For example, if you believe in feeding on demand and your nurse insists on putting your baby on a schedule, if you're planning on breast-feeding and your nurse thinks the bottle is a better option, or if you're looking for a teacher but your nurse wants total control, you're asking for trouble.

Finding the right baby nurse is extremely important if you plan on breast-feeding. Nursing your baby can be very frustrating until you (and your baby) have become used to it, so if you intend to breast-feed you'll want a nurse who is experienced and supportive in helping both mother and baby get started.

One mother of our acquaintance had difficulty starting; she says she probably would have given up if it hadn't been for her baby nurse. The baby nurse worked with her for days—applying warm compresses to prevent her breasts from becoming engorged, massaging to help the milk flow, showing her how to use the baby's own rooting instincts to find the breast, constantly encouraging her, and telling her that her goal was worth all the trouble and frustration. In short, the nurse simply wouldn't let her give up—until finally both mother and child were comfortable and happy nursing.

While our friend had a good experience, her cousin (who had similar problems getting started) had a bad one. She had an unsympathetic nurse, whom she soon dismissed, and with no one around to help and encourage her, she grew too frustrated to continue and gave up breast-feeding.

HOW TO FIND A BABY NURSE

Many parents find their baby nurses through the reputable baby
nurse agencies located in most major metropolitan areas. If you
don't live in a city but you are able to provide transportation, a nurse
hired through an agency may travel to you. Agencies generally do at
least some screening of their nurses, but while nurses are often
qualified L.P.N.s or even R.N.s, others receive their training from
the agency itself. Still others have minimal training, if any at all. So
although agencies do a preliminary screening, it's really up to you to
find a nurse you trust and who best suits your needs.

If you don't want to use an agency (or don't have one you consider
reputable in your area), there are a lot of other ways to find baby
nurses:

- Ask your pediatrician or the head nurse in the pediatrics unit of
  your hospital for a referral.

- Call a local nurses' registry (not childcare).

- Look at the bulletin board or ask the salesperson at the store
  where you bought your layette. (One mother we know found
  her baby nurse in a baby store—while she was waiting to pay, a
  nurse who was out buying clothes for the infant currently in her
  charge handed her card to the owner of the store.)

- Speak to your Lamaze instructor or listen to the neighborhood
  or family grapevine.

- Look in the yellow pages.

- Possibly the best method is to get referrals from friends; they'll
  tell you more of what you need to know than you could ever
  learn from an anonymous reference. (Many highly competent

nurses work through individual referrals only; if you know of one by all means consider her.)

In short, there are a lot of ways to get a baby nurse. The real question is how do you get a good one? Dr. Judy Goldstein says, "It's really trial and error. The agencies aren't as trustworthy as you'd like them to be. Try to determine for yourself the baby nurse's nurturing approach."

You may find a great baby nurse, but if she's someone who works on her own rather than through an agency, you could be taking a chance—if your baby is early or late she may have other commitments. Be sure to check on her reliability and availability as well as her qualifications; ask her how she books her time and what system she employs for honoring her commitments.

The question of whether a baby nurse will be there when you need her is perhaps the most definite advantage of working through an agency: Because an agency may employ scores of nurses, alternate arrangements can be made if your baby is early or late and the nurse of your choice is working on another job. (Of course, you have no guarantees that the substitute sent by the agency will meet your needs.)

Also, because there is no licensing procedure for baby nurses, you may feel you're more likely to find a nurse with a certain level of competence and training when you work through an established agency; at least you have a greater choice and if you don't like one you can ask the agency to send someone else for an interview.

Executives at Avalon and other agencies suggest that potential clients call well in advance of the due date. They then ask parents these preliminary questions:

• Due date? (This helps them determine their schedule; they will arrange contingencies even if delivery is a little early or late.)

- Age of mother? (Ease of delivery and speed of recovery is determined to some extent by the mother's age and physical condition.)

- Expected method of delivery? (C-section moms take longer to recover and need more physical help.)

- Other children? (Will they need supervision and care from the nurse? If so, agencies may charge more money.)

- Other household help? (Again, this helps them figure out how much physical work is involved; if a housekeeper cleans and takes care of older children, it means fewer chores for the nurse.)

- Sleeping arrangements? (Where a nurse sleeps—nursery, living room, or guest room—has a lot to do with her comfort and working conditions.)

- Pets? (Some nurses are allergic, others believe infants should not be exposed to animals.)

- Cigarettes? (If you smoke and the nurse does not, or vice versa, the situation probably won't work.)

- Services expected and required? (Special needs and personal preferences help an agency determine which nurse they should send to you.)

After speaking with expectant parents on the phone, the agency will recommend a specific nurse (or nurses). But families are not expected to hire simply on the basis of an agency referral. Just like you, baby nurses have different personalities and ways of doing things. You want to find a nurse you like and trust, and the way to find the right person—whether she's come to you through an agency or a friend—is through an interview. In most cases, parents will interview nurses in their own home (sometimes preceded by a telephone interview) about two months before the baby is due.

Some agencies only send one nurse, others send two; but *if you're not satisfied after an interview, ask to see someone else.* And if you're not happy with the quality of people sent to you by an agency, you are under no obligation to hire anyone. Look elsewhere; your baby is worth all your time and trouble, even if it takes ten interviews to find the person you like and trust.

We asked both parents and nurses what they would look for in a baby nurse and what questions they would ask if they were interviewing for a nurse. Here are some questions, divided into categories, as well as some general guidelines on how to interpret answers. (You would not be asking all these questions; the interview would take all day. Ask what's most important to you.)

INTERVIEWING THE BABY NURSE

Try to help the prospective employee relax while getting a feel for who she is—her general attitude, personality, and competence. Without directly asking, you might ascertain whether you can get along with her—is she flexible, can she respond to your needs, do her ideas about the job coincide with your own. And remember, while you're checking her out, she's checking you out, too—she might ask where she'll sleep, where she'll eat, whether you smoke, and what *you* expect of her. She doesn't have to accept a job from you, even if you offer it.

Background Questions

How did you become interested in being a baby nurse?

Why do you do this work?

How long have you done it?

What are your qualifications? Training?

Tell us about some of the babies you've worked with.

Are there any particularly good experiences you might share with us?

Any bad experiences?

Tell us about the mother in your experience who needed the most help.

Child Handling

The way you word these questions is very important; they are not only about skills, but about biases as well. To get honest responses, not those the nurse thinks you want to hear, phrase questions in a neutral manner.

When do you use a pacifier?

How would you work with a breast-feeding mom?

How do you handle the baby's feeding schedule?

What do you do when a baby has gas? Fever? Cradle cap?

What about an emergency?

Do you know cardiopulmonary resuscitation (CPR)?

What do you do for a baby who cries all the time? A baby who won't sleep?

Do you prefer boy babies or girl babies? Why?

At what point would you suggest calling a pediatrician?

What kind of diapers do you like?

When you change a baby, do you use lotion? Powder? Anything?

Tell us about how you bathe a newborn.

Do you always sterilize baby bottles or can you use a dishwasher?

What about visitors? Taking the baby outside?

Personal Habits and Requirements

What do you need and what does the baby nurse need? These kinds of questions have to do with compatibility, both in terms of conditions of employment and personality.

Do you smoke? Would you be opposed to us or our guests smoking?

Should pets be kept away from the baby?

Do you wear a uniform?

In handling the baby, when is it necessary to wash your hands? (Before feeding? After changing? Before changing?) In general, how important is cleanliness to you?

What hours are you willing to work?

Will you work every day, or do you expect days off?

Will you get up in the middle of the night?

Will you sit with the mother at night?

If you have the time, will you run some errands or straighten up?

What sleeping arrangements do you prefer/require?

How much will you use the telephone? Watch television?

Do you expect to eat with the family?

Will you prepare your own meals?

Philosophy

Ask yourself some questions first: Do you want someone who will take charge or someone who will take orders, a person who's organized or one who's spontaneous, a teacher or a doer? Ask the nurse questions that help you determine whether her ideas and attitudes are right for you.

Should feeding be on a schedule or on demand?

Which is better, breast-feeding or bottle feeding?

Should a baby be picked up as soon as he cries, or should he cry it out?

What will I do while you're here? Should I rest? Feed the baby?

Will you always change the diapers?

What's the father's role with a newborn?

What about grandparents? Other visitors?

How would you introduce other children to the new baby?

What experiences have you had with pediatricians?

What's the difference between boys and girls?

What about adopted children? Single parents?

Do you think of yourself as a teacher?

What do you consider to be your responsibilities in this job?

Everyone we spoke with agreed that even if you respond to someone in a personal interview it's essential to get and check references; you're not infallible and a referral by an agency does not ensure competence or emotional stability. When checking references, it's important to determine not only whether the reference was satisfied with the baby nurse's work, but what her views on nurturing are, what her needs were, etc. Just because the nurse was right for someone else doesn't mean she will be for you. (For more on checking references, see chapter 4.)

So now it's done: You've finally asked all your questions and checked all her references. How do you make your decision? In the end, it's based on whether you like the person, whether you trust her, and whether you feel you can live with her and learn from her in the first weeks of your child's life.

TERMS OF EMPLOYMENT FOR BABY NURSES

A newborn baby sleeps most of the day, but your baby nurse is on call all the time and should not be expected to perform an infinite number of tasks not directly concerned with the care of the baby and the mother. Generally, nurses who sleep in get four hours off for each twenty-four hours on call; she needs to rest (even when on call) and you should do your best to arrange a private place for her. (Most of the nurses we spoke with preferred setting up in the nursery rather than sleeping on a couch in the living room; they felt it gave them more privacy.) The co-owners of the Fox Agency in New York City (which was started in 1936) told us that "some nurses sleep when the baby sleeps—and particularly if it's a colicky baby, the nurse thinks it's unfair for the mother to ask her to do something extra during that sleep time."

A baby nurse may or may not have days off; if you want her to work on Sunday, make it clear at the very beginning (before you actually need her). Otherwise you may find you're in a tug of war, when all that you really want is peace and tranquility.

Baby nurses in general are well paid, whether you pay them directly or through an agency. Unlike permanent childcare workers, they are paid in a fee-for-service arrangement and on a per diem basis; that means you pay them for the days they actually work and you take no taxes out of their check.

You are not responsible for paying the baby nurse for any time she does not work. Even if you've indicated you want her to stay for two weeks, and you later decide you can get by on your own after the first week, you can let her go at that time without having to pay her for the second week. (If you feel like it, and you've let her go because of your own needs—rather than fired her with cause—you may want to give her an extra day's pay.)

Depending on the circumstances, a baby nurse generally stays for a week or two, occasionally longer. Usually by then parents are relatively comfortable with their child, the mother is fairly well recovered from childbirth (even from a C-section), and it's time to go it alone or with permanent help.

ASKING A BABY NURSE TO STAY ON

If you ask her, your baby nurse may agree to stay. But be careful; although this arrangement sometimes works out, it's more often problematical. The job of a baby nurse is very different from that of a permanent care giver, both on an emotional, nurturing level and physically. It's not by chance that people choose to be baby nurses. In general, they don't want to become attached to children in the way permanent care givers do. They come and go; many of them want to avoid emotional involvement, preferring to leave before the baby is old enough to really respond to them as individuals. Also, as Dr. Carol Livoti said, "A baby nurse has to get up in the middle of the night. A person who takes care of a three-year-old needs to be talkative and empathetic."

The baby nurse's relationship with a baby is primarily physical (although with you it may be psychological). Baby nurses are often older women, many of whom are simply unable to keep up with an active toddler. In addition, many permanent care givers also do some housework, errands, and other homemaking tasks, and baby nurses do virtually none.

FIRING A BABY NURSE

Of course there are objective reasons for firing a baby nurse, principally having to do with incompetence and unwillingness to do what the job requires. But these aren't the only reasons. If you've just come home from the hospital with your baby, you don't need a person around who makes you uncomfortable. So please, if for any reason you feel you want to fire a baby nurse—whether it's because she's handling your baby in a way you don't like or because she's simply driving you crazy—don't be reluctant to do so. And once you've made the decision to ask her to leave, act decisively; you don't need to give notice to someone who's only expecting to work two weeks, so make sure she leaves immediately. (For more information on how to dismiss a care giver, see chapter 8.)

If you let somebody go whom you've hired through an agency and you still want a baby nurse, you should contact the agency immediately. Whatever the reason for the dismissal—whether it was for incompetence or simply because her ideas or personality didn't mesh with your own—a reputable agency will try to find a replacement.

Although some people do have bad experiences with baby nurses, it's definitely more the exception than the rule. A successful baby nurse is one who learns to adapt to the circumstances and needs of the many families for whom she works, and one who is unable to adapt does not usually remain in the business very long.

If you're careful about hiring and you make your wants and needs clear, you will most likely have a positive experience. Then, like so many of the mothers we spoke with, you will always remember your baby nurse as the sympathetic helper who contributed to making the first weeks of your baby's life a truly joyful experience.

CHAPTER 3

Choosing and Finding the Right Kind of Care for Your Child

Once you become a parent many of the clichés about parenthood stop being clichés—they become realities. Your life changes radically; your child becomes a central focus of your thoughts and dreams; caring for a child really is a tremendous amount of work; your children's small triumphs and accomplishments can in fact loom larger than Olympic victories. Another cliché (which is not really a cliché) is *until you have your own child you can't know what you really want and need in the way of childcare.* All the good planning in the world can't prepare you adequately for the reality of the new person with whom you now share your life.

- A mother may fully expect to go back to work full-time before her baby is six weeks old, but having an infant to hold in her arms often changes her plans.

29

- A family may feel that the husband's income alone will be sufficient for them to live with their new baby for an extended period of time, but in fact the increased costs of having a child may force the mother back to work long before she planned.

- A couple may expect to hire live-in help, but after two weeks with a baby nurse they just might decide that their privacy is more important than the convenience of having someone there all the time.

The reality is that there are innumerable instances where financial or physical realities differ from expectations, and just as many instances where, totally unexpectedly, compelling emotional responses force changes in plans.

Fortunately, you can modify your expectations and you can change your plans. There is no standard contract you have with your child except to love and care for him or her, and there is no one way to arrange your childcare.

DIFFERENT NEEDS, DIFFERENT ARRANGEMENTS

Among the hundreds of families we interviewed for this book, we found a striking diversity in childcare arrangements. What was right for one family was totally wrong for another. What works for the people next door won't necessarily work for you. And what works for you with your first child may stop working when your child gets a little older or has a brother or sister.

You may want your childcare person to wash the breakfast dishes; your neighbors may not eat breakfast. You may require someone to cook and clean as well as take care of your children; the folks across the street may hire a second person to clean the house. An urban family may need someone who can negotiate the neighborhood and the public transportation system; a suburban or rural family will probably require a care giver who can drive a car. The differences between families' needs and expectations of childcare workers involve time, duties, and skills—virtually every facet of the job.

There is no one set way of arranging in-home childcare. The reality is that there are almost as many childcare solutions as there are childcare situations. Remember, your solution is unique, entirely your own. Don't make your decisions based on what works for someone else. Your best solution answers a simple question: What works for you?

A SAMPLING OF CHILDCARE SOLUTIONS

We know one family where the mother works part time (three days a week). Their childcare employee comes to work Monday morning at 8:00 and lives in until Friday night; from Monday to Wednesday her principal duties are those of a care giver, but because of the mother's schedule, on Thursday and Friday she functions primarily as a housekeeper.

In a suburban family where both parents are professionals, on call twenty-four hours a day, the arrangement involves two people: a primary care giver who comes at 8:00 A.M. and leaves at 6:00 P.M., five days a week and a college student who takes over at 6:00 and is responsible through the night (in the parents' absence) in return for room and board.

A working-class couple from a small New England town, both of whom worked the night shift, found that the solution that best fit their needs was to hire responsible local high-school students to stay with their children in the evenings. This allowed them the freedom to work, and cost them far less than hiring a more mature care giver.

An urban professional couple, both of whom work long hours, hired two overlapping full-time people. The "morning-afternoon" care giver accompanies the kids on organized activities, arranges play dates, and takes care of lunch. The "afternoon-evening" care giver does the cleaning, cooks and feeds the kids dinner, and, when necessary, puts them to bed at night.

A Boston family employs several people: a woman who works daily from 8:00 to 4:00 whose duties include childcare and light housecleaning; a college student who comes every Monday evening and another who comes every Thursday, each working from 6:30 to 10:30 P.M.; and a baby sitter/cleaning person who works four to eight hours each weekend.

A New York family shares a full-time (9:00 to 5:30) care giver with another family; the employee is the primary care giver in one household three days a week and functions similarly for the other the remaining two days. Each family also hires a once-a-week cleaning woman.

In another New York family, once their youngest child went to school they no longer needed (nor could they afford) full-time childcare. Their solution was to have their housekeeper split her time between their home and their neighbors', watching the children of both families after school and cleaning both homes on alternate days.

In a New Jersey family with a full-time mom, the solution was to hire a student to come in after school as a mother's helper, thus allowing the mother a couple of hours of free time to herself each weekday.

A Chicago mother told us about her arrangement, "My two co-workers and I jointly hired a care giver to care for our three girls, all one to two years old, in my apartment. It was a *wonderful* arrangement because the children had each other and a home environment and a reliable care giver. The mothers also all knew and trusted each other and took joint responsibility."

A Connecticut family employs a live-in who works 8:00 to 6:00 Monday through Friday plus one night a week and one Saturday night a month.

So as you see, your choices for "how" to arrange childcare are virtually unlimited—and the choices are entirely yours.

Now let's approach the "who" of in-home childcare with some definitions. The first thing to understand is that these definitions are far from hard and fast: These job titles are simply a convenient way of describing "general" differences. Two people called "housekeepers" may have completely different duties—in fact whether we're talking about a nanny, a babysitter, or an au pair, the terms of employment, days and hours worked, and salaries vary according to the individual family situation.

SOME WORKING DEFINITIONS FOR CHILDCARE EMPLOYERS

Nanny

Strictly speaking, nanny is a very specific term for a person who is formally educated as a childcare worker. As defined in the Delta College (University Center, Michigan) Nanny Program brochure, "A nanny is a trained in-home childcare professional who works as part of a family team to provide for the child's physical, emotional, educational, social and recreational needs."

The classic English nanny has been certified by Britain's National Nursery Examination Board. The "nanny" course of study is much like that of a two-year technical college; after high school, starting at about age sixteen, students are trained in childcare as a profession; graduates are qualified to work in daycare centers or hospital nurseries, nursery schools or preschools, as well as in private homes. Three of the most well-known private nanny-training schools in England are Norland Nursery Training College, Chiltern Nursery Training College, and Princess Christian College.

A number of American nanny schools have recently opened that offer similar, although generally not as extensive, courses in child-care. Some of these schools are accredited by the American Council of Nanny Schools (see appendix C). Typically, in both England and America, a nanny has taken courses in health and nutrition, child development, and child safety.

People in America often think of nannies as very proper servants in white uniforms; actually the modern nanny wears whatever she's comfortable in, anything from blue jeans to a skirt and blouse. Her relationship with a family can be "properly distant" or warm and informal—it all depends on the personalities and preferences of the nanny and the members of the family.

As for what she does, Wilma, a British nanny who is now work-ing in America, told us, "A nanny teaches children; she's somewhere in between a governess and a housekeeper. Most nannies today crawl around on the floor with the children."

One thing nannies do not do is general housework; they do, however, cook, clean, and do the laundry for the children in their charge. Like dietitians and many other skilled workers, they con-sider themselves skilled professionals. As Wilma said, "I'm there to stimulate the children. I didn't go to college for two years to learn how to vacuum."

In America, most nannies live in but we did interview a few who live out. Most work full-time (which can often extend to as much as a twelve-hour day), but some will sign on for part-time work. In England most nannies work full time and live out.

Because of their training, nannies command the highest salaries of all home childcare workers.

Childcare Person (Care Giver)

Like a nanny, a care giver's primary task is caring for children. The most significant difference between a care giver and a nanny is that the care giver hasn't gone to school for the job. She may have a lifetime of experience in caring for children or her qualifications may be nothing more than taking care of her younger brother or sister. Unlike a nanny, a care giver may also do some general housekeeping tasks. Childcare work is her profession; she is in most cases an adult and a permanent employee.

Au Pair

Connie Crosson, former New York regional director of Au Pair Homestay USA (which places foreign au pairs in American homes through the U.S. Information Agency), says, "*Au pair* means 'on par with' the family—they are like a cousin, niece, or nephew coming to help the mother. Au pairs should take total care of the child and they can straighten up but not clean unless it's a family activity (like washing windows on Saturday afternoon). They are not to feel they are servants."

Many of these girls and boys have taken a childcare job because they want to travel and learn about new places. As a result, sometimes they're much more interested in exploring their new surroundings than they are in working. As one mother who has used au pairs told us, "They're adolescents, and they're going to do age-appropriate things. They're not going to act like adults." Another spoke of "the problems of being 'surrogate parents' to a nineteen-year-old from another culture."

Whatever the specifics of your relationship with an au pair, you, as the employer, are responsible both for decisions about their teenage concerns (such as use of the family car) and for your own expectations about what they will do for you. In addition, because au pairs live in with your family you are responsible for their welfare.

Realistically, au pairs can make terrific mother's helpers. Because they are generally quite young (eighteen to twenty-one) and inexperienced, they may be better suited to families with preschool or school-age children than to those with infants and toddlers.

Au pairs tend to be from Europe or rural areas of the U.S. West and Midwest. Some European au pairs come in through programs such as Au Pair Homestay USA or a similar U.S. Information Agency–sponsored program, the Au Pair in America program. Other foreign au pairs are found through advertising in international or European newspapers or personal references. (Those employed through Au Pair Homestay USA are required to do some schoolwork, even if it's just a once-a-week potter's course— and their visas are issued specifically for this educational-cultural exchange.) Other foreign au pairs have work permits and visas that allow them to remain in the United States legally for a limited period of time, typically from three months to a year. Many come in under student visas; many, whose visas have expired, are here illegally. (For more information about immigration laws see chapter 10.)

American au pairs don't require visas, but because of regional differences they may have a cultural perspective that's very different from your own. For example, a Salt Lake City–based organization called Helpers West places Mormon au pairs in New York–area homes. Evidently many families think they're better off hiring a Mormon au pair (because of the strong church policy against drinking, smoking, and premarital sex) than a teenager whose upbringing is more mainstream or liberal.

Baby Sitter

"Baby sitter" is a term often used interchangeably with care giver, but our definition is of someone who comes into your home on an *ad hoc* basis to watch your children for several hours. This person, who is not a permanent employee, may be a teenager or an older person. He or she is not a childcare professional.

Mother's Helper

Girls and boys who act as mother's helpers are sort of quasi–baby sitters or local au pairs. Like au pairs, mother's helpers are not permanent childcare employees. They are teenagers hired for a limited period of time who assist mothers in taking care of children. They often act as baby sitters for families who take extended summer vacations; they may also come on a regular basis after school to watch the kids and keep them busy. Those who join a family for a summer at the beach are paid in room and board, a modicum of free time and a little money; those who live at home are generally paid on an hourly basis in much the same way as evening baby sitters.

Governess

There aren't too many governesses around anymore. If you're very well off, travel frequently, and take your children along (thus preventing regular school attendance), or if you live in Kuwait and don't find the schools to your liking, you may choose to hire a governess. A governess is an in-home tutor, in charge of a child's education as well as well-being. By way of comparison, a nanny is somewhere between a governess and a baby sitter.

Housekeeper

A housekeeper is a person hired to manage your house. She cleans, cooks, shops, does the laundry, the ironing, and other housework. She may do some child-related chores such as picking up your children from school and transporting them to other activities. The term "housekeeper" is often used interchangeably with care giver, but used in that way, it's not a terribly accurate or precise job title.

Many parents told us that whatever term they used to describe their childcare person, children, particularly those of school age, invariably refer to her as "my baby sitter." While we can list the advantages and disadvantages of each type of arrangement, the comparisons might be misleading because many childcare people refer to themselves as "baby sitters," for example, but function by the definition of nannies.

There is one area, however, where we think listing the pros and cons can help—and that's in your choice of live-in versus live-out help.

LIVE-IN/LIVE-OUT HELP

First the definitions. *Live-in* simply means someone who lives in your home. *Live-out,* on the other hand, is someone who goes to her own home during the hours and days when she's not working.

Advantages of Live-In Help

- Childcare is readily accessible. A baby sitter is always there when you need her.

- No transportation requirements.

- Minimal use/abuse of sick days.

- Allows for parents to have a flexible work schedule.

Advantages of Live-Out Help

- Families have more privacy. Your baby sitter is not around when you'd rather be with your children by yourselves.

- No need to provide housing and amenities (television, telephone, bathroom, etc.).

- Less involvement in the intimate details of a baby sitter's personal life. Parents are more readily able to maintain the employer-employee relationship.

- Parents' responsibility toward the baby sitter ends at the end of her working day. If she is sick, she takes care of herself. Her social life and physical needs are taken care of on her own time and without involving you.

When it comes to taking care of your children you want someone who's warm, loving, responsible, and kind. But there are other criteria. So before you go out to look for a permanent care giver it's important to have your own job description clear in your mind: This includes, but is not limited to, hours, duties, your child's needs, and your needs. You design the job; you're in control and you should know what you want.

Often a mother and father disagree; it's important to work this out between yourselves. (And if grandparents live with you, to work it out with them as well.) There will always be trade-offs in making this kind of decision; no one can be just like you, and no one is perfect (even you). You must decide which qualities in a care giver are most important to you. So how do you know what you want and need? Here are a few suggestions.

DETERMINING YOUR CHILDCARE NEEDS

To help you determine what kind of childcare is best for you:

- Ask other people with similar family situations what works best for them.

- Stay home yourself; put yourself in a care giver's shoes and see what the job actually involves.

- Carefully analyze your particular requirements and financial situation in order to make a realistic appraisal.

In determining your childcare needs, you will want to think about a whole range of variables, including:

- Both the ages and number of your children.

- Your work schedule.

- Your children's schedules (including school vacations).

- Your need to have them brought to or picked up from school or other activities.

- Your budget.

- The amount of space you have in your home.

- The availability of transportation.

- Your housekeeping requirements.

- Even your philosophy of child rearing.

Let's go over a few of these variables to see what we're talking about. The most important mesh in a childcare relationship is between child and care giver, but you, as responsible parents, make the hiring decisions that make it work for your child.

If you have a very young infant, you need someone who will be totally responsible and responsive. Babies are completely dependent on the people who care for them. Above all else, you want to hire someone who will provide love and nurturing affection to your baby; she should also be able to deal with emergencies, and you should be able to trust her—unequivocally. Because babies sleep more than older children and aren't as physically demanding, an older, grandmotherly person may be perfectly fine at this age.

If you have an older infant, you will probably want someone who will stimulate your baby, who will respond to your baby's signals— smiling, laughter, or tears—and who will give your baby a sense of security in your absence. Because infants after the first few months have strong attachments to particular people, and those relationships become more difficult to form after about the sixth month, it's best to hire someone before your baby reaches this stage. You may be able to ask a younger care giver to do more housework than you could an older person at this time, but even now, your baby is very demanding of time and attention. And whatever the energy level of your care giver, when your child reaches toddler stage it may well become unrealistic to expect an immaculate house *and* a content and stimulated child.

If you have a toddler, you need someone who will encourage your child to explore and experience, who will reassure him, and who will keep him safe from harm. Your toddler may be capable of turning on the stove long before he understands that fire is dangerous. A care giver for a toddler thus must have the capability of both providing encouragement and protection—and she must be ever vigilant as well as infinitely patient.

If you have a preschooler, you need a care giver who can keep up with his boundless curiosity, enthusiasm, and energy; someone who can play with your child and help him develop his skills and imagination. In addition, you'll probably want someone who can arrange and supervise activities with other children and who's social enough herself to encourage healthy peer interaction and mediate squabbles. And because your child at this age is really still part baby and part child, you'll want a person who can help him develop as a social being.

If you have a school-age child, you may need a care giver to feed him, dress him properly, get him to school and back home, and encourage him in schoolwork and safe play.

If you have more than one child, you may need someone who can combine the traits and abilities of the above categories and who is able to divide her energies so that all the children get what they need.

If you have a child with special needs, you may need someone with unique skills or special training. A handicapped child may require even more encouragement and empathy than other children, and in your absence, you want someone who can give him what he needs. If your special needs child has brothers or sisters, your ideal child-care person will also be able to take care of them, both emotionally and physically, and will help allow you to provide for all your children's needs.

Based on your understanding of your own children, you may choose a nanny, a care giver, or a housekeeper. You may also have to decide whether you want someone calm or energetic, someone young or someone older (a sixty-five-year-old might be great with an immobile infant but has a terrible time keeping up with an energetic toddler on a tricycle), someone athletic or someone who will spend hours reading to your child, and someone whose style is highly structured or someone totally improvisational.

You will also need to answer questions about discipline: Do you feel more comfortable about a person with a laissez-faire attitude toward discipline or someone who is a firm disciplinarian? Do you prefer a care giver to respond as she sees fit or do you demand that no disciplinary action be taken without always speaking to you first?

In the end, you want someone who, in your absence, can respond to your child in a way that you feel good about. Who that person should be depends to the largest extent not just on practical considerations, but on who your child is and what your values are.

WHAT ABOUT YOUR NEEDS?

Consider Your Employment Situation and Financial Condition

Do both parents work? Full time or part time? Or is yours a single-working-parent household? What are your hours of work? If your hours are in any way unusual you may need someone who is willing to work extraordinary hours.

What is your family income? What can you afford to pay for childcare? Considering your family budget, what kind of arrangement can you best afford?

One New York City mother we spoke with works three full days a week; she considered hiring someone as a baby sitter on an hourly basis at approximately $50 a day, but instead decided that for $225 a week she could hire someone full time as a combination care giver-housekeeper. For her, the extra $75 a week was affordable and worthwhile; it allowed her to spend her free time with her child rather than having to cook and clean.

A New Jersey family with another part-time working mother came up with a totally different solution. They had a relatively tight budget and a large house; their decision was to hire an au pair, whose salary is lower than other care givers and whose room and board was less expensive for them than the difference in salary. Like these two examples, you may be able to find a way to stretch your budget to suit your needs.

Many people we spoke with didn't want any doubt in their care givers' minds about their primary function; these families, finances permitting, employed separate people to clean their homes. And several mothers we interviewed who don't work outside the home have part-time care givers so they can do other things.

By being flexible about childcare arrangements, people of moderate means are not excluded from an in-home solution. You don't have to be rich to afford in-home childcare.

What role do you want and expect your care giver to take in child rearing and in your home?

What will be her objective childcare duties?

Transporting children to and from school or other activities. (Will she need to drive?)

Changing diapers.

Bathing children.

Cooking for and feeding children.

Arranging play dates.

Participating with child in organized activities (art and music, gym and swimming classes).

Putting children to bed at night.

Waking them and dressing them in the morning.

Shopping for children's toys and clothes.

Taking children to doctor or dentist.

What role do you want her to take in your child's upbringing?

How much initiative do you want her to take in terms of activities, in terms of discipline?

Do you want someone who's nurturing?

Do you want her to be a teacher? (In this context, consider the importance of her level of literacy and English-language skills.)

Do you want a playmate for your child?

How attentive should she be?

How important is it that her child-rearing philosophy match yours?

What will be her housekeeping duties?
Food shopping

General errands

Laundry

Ironing

Cooking

Washing dishes

Vacuuming

Light cleaning

Heavy cleaning

Taking care of pets

Remember, the more you ask in terms of housework, the less you can expect in terms of childcare. A care giver who is asked to wash the floors may plop the kids down in front of the television so that she can do her work uninterrupted. If you want someone to teach and constantly attend to your child, you can't expect her to do the heavy cleaning as well. You set the priorities.

What will be her working conditions?
This question encompasses an extremely wide range of issues. The first of these issues is invariably salary; before you begin, you should determine to the best of your ability how much you are willing and able to pay.

Next are general workers' benefits. For example, will you pay her sick leave, and if so, how much? Will she receive a paid vacation? If so, how much time will you give her, and will she be given the option as to when she takes her vacation? In order to be sure of their care giver's availability when they need her, many families insist that she take her vacation at the same time they are taking their own. This, however, must be done with a sense of fairness. One New York family we know spent the summer in Europe. They didn't pay their care giver for six of the eight weeks they were away and were surprised when they came home and learned that she had found a new job.

An additional benefit you may want to consider is medical insurance. One family, for example, after their care giver had been employed by them for a year, put her on their group medical plan and paid for her insurance.

What are the hours and days you expect her to work? This is a very important issue, and it's something you should be aware of before you begin the process of hiring.

Will she be working on-the-books or off? This is not simply a question of law (although according to law you and your household employee are subject to various taxes and tax benefits); in reality many parents find it more "convenient" to pay their childcare people off-the-books. But if you are paying your care giver on-the-books as the law requires, you will be deducting for social security (you pay half and she pays half), you will be paying for unemployment insurance benefits, and in some states you are required by law to provide worker's compensation benefits as well.

How far do you expect your care giver to travel to and from work? (If it's more than an hour each way and the hours of work are long, it may put an undue strain on your care giver.)

Do you want someone who will live in or live out? (If you want a childcare person to live in, do you have the room and can you ensure the privacy that will allow the arrangement to work?)

There are a host of other questions about working conditions, and these vary according to each family's particular requirements.

Will she be expected to travel with the family?

Will she be allowed visitors?

On her days off, will you need her to be on call or on premises?

Will she be allowed to use the family car, and, if so, under what circumstances?

Will she eat with the family? Will she be expected to provide her own food?

There are many other possible issues you may have to deal with concerning your care giver's working conditions. Figuring out what's important and what needs to be spelled out is your responsibility, both as parents and as employers.

PARENTS' AND CARE GIVERS' EXPECTATIONS

Parents' expectations of care givers vary widely. Some expect the world; others are more realistic. Here are some selected responses concerning expectations that we received to our questionnaires and in our interviews with parents.

• "I want my nanny to be a substitute mother for my children."

- "I want her to be half servant, half sister."

- "She should be more than an employee. I want her to be part of the family."

- "I just want someone who'll love and take care of my child."

- "We want someone who's professional, intelligent, and warm."

- "I can't tolerate an uppity baby sitter. She must be subservient."

We also distributed a questionnaire to care givers. Here are some of their responses.

- "They treat you like a handmaid. You have to come any time they call. Parents should treat us like human beings."

- "This is just a job."

- "They think baby-sitting is all you can do, that you can't do anything else in your life."

- "I wish we could be more respected. This is the truth."

Parents should be realistic about their expectations for a childcare worker. What in fact are realistic expectations? Let's start with the most obvious fact: To you, it's your home and your child, but to your care giver, it's a job.

If the job brings attachment, love, and respect, generally everyone (especially your children) benefits. It's no coincidence that virtually every care giver told us about the need for respect, and that the vast majority of parents who were satisfied with their permanent child-care arrangements also spoke about their relationships of mutual respect with caregivers.

You may expect yourself to be on call twenty-four hours a day, but you cannot reasonably expect this of your employee. You may give selflessly to your children, but your care giver (who may in fact love your kids) may also have a family of her own.

YOUR ROLE AS PARENT AND EMPLOYER

Every pediatrician, parenting expert, and child psychologist we spoke with emphasized that any relationship between parent and care giver must always remain one of employer and employee. Although you can, and should, expect mutual respect and even hope for love between your child and his caretaker, you can never make her part of your family. The simple fact is that she's not a member of your family, that no matter how long she works for you and how much love and respect you and your children share with her, she will always be your employee, taking care of *your* children. She is dependent on you for the food she puts on her table, but she also has a life of her own that is separate from your family's.

The noted developmental psychologist Dr. Irving Sigel of the Educational Testing Service thinks many working mothers feel guilty about leaving their children in someone else's care. To them a family member feels like a more acceptable substitute, so if they can make their childcare employee into "one of the family" they may be able to ease their own pain at separation.

However, your children's well-being is your responsibility. If you become overly familiar or intimate with your children's care giver, you may well be blurring the distinctions between yourself as parent and employer and the care giver as worker. You will be complicating the basic employer-employee relationship and undermining your authority. It's very hard to tell your sister or your best friend that she's doing something that you don't approve of.

HOW TO FIND HELP

You know what kind of childcare you want—you've thought through your children's particular needs (and your own), your means, your desires. Your best possible childcare situation is firmly in your mind. Now, how and where in the world do you find someone who fits the bill?

In all likelihood, she won't fall into your lap, although it would be wonderful if she did. You have to look. There are many ways of finding a childcare worker. Here are some of the time-honored methods.

Word of Mouth

Put the word out—to friends, family, acquaintances, and co-workers. Use your entire social network: your place of worship; your office; and any social, political, or professional organizations you may belong to. Ask everyone you know to ask their friends; ask friends who are parents to ask their own childcare people.

We know of one mother who belonged to a professional women's association; she called everyone listed in the organization's membership directory, trying to elicit someone who could recommend a care giver. Eventually her networking paid off.

Another family, whose au pair was returning to her native country, was having difficulty finding an acceptable replacement—until they mentioned their plight to some members of their synagogue one Saturday after services. It just so happened that a member of their congregation had a long-term childcare employee who was no longer needed. She was warm, loving, intelligent, responsive, and responsible—everything the family that was searching could hope for in a care giver. And she had the best of references—seven years in the home of someone known to the parents.

It's also possible to find people through care giver networks. Ask your friends and their childcare people for recommendations; very often care givers have friends and relatives who, for one reason or another, are looking for jobs. If you make sure you get details on how well the care giver knows the person she's referring, her strong recommendation is as trustworthy as any. (However, as you would anytime you hire a care giver, you should be certain to check other references—the childcare person may be recommending her needy, and altogether unqualified, sister-in-law.)

It's not easy to find someone through word of mouth; it may even take months and if you don't have the time it might not be worth the wait. But because you know the people who are making the recommendations and can check back with them, it's usually the most reliable method of finding someone good.

Bulletin Boards

Bulletin boards are located in children's bookstores, pediatricians' offices, libraries, supermarkets, community centers, churches, synagogues, hospital nurseries, colleges, nursery schools—virtually anywhere. Here are a couple of examples of good bulletin board notices.

WARM, LOVING, RESPONSIBLE PERSON NEEDED
TO CARE FOR BOY AND GIRL AGES 4 AND 7
MON.–FRI. 8:30–6:00
ENGLISH NATIVE LANGUAGE
NO SMOKING
LOVES PETS
LIGHT HOUSEWORK
REFERENCES REQUIRED
(PHONE NUMBER WITH TAGS)

CHILDCARE/HOUSEKEEPER

BRIGHT, ENERGETIC, EXPERIENCED
FOR FAMILY WITH 2-YEAR-OLD GIRL
LIVE-IN
(OWN ROOM WITH BATH, TV)
DRIVER'S LICENSE
REFERENCES
MUST HAVE GREEN CARD OR U.S. CITIZENSHIP
(PHONE NUMBER WITH TAGS)

In order to maximize responses, you'll want to put your notices wherever a potential care giver may see them. In addition, many areas now have video or cable television bulletin boards; you may want to look into these as well.

Newspaper Advertising

This encompasses everything from the classified ad section of a major metropolitan newspaper to a local paper for a special audience (including ethnic-oriented papers) to alumni and company newsletters, church or synagogue bulletins, and free community papers. (In both New York's the *Irish Echo* and the *New York Times* you'll find numerous out-of-town ads—don't assume you won't get responses from a classified ad placed in a periodical in another city. There are some papers that pull in *national* advertising for household employment.) In addition, some people find au pairs and other care givers by advertising in newspapers in foreign countries or in areas of this country where many au pairs come from (for example, the *Salt Lake City Tribune* in Utah or the *Minneapolis Star Tribune* in Minnesota).

Newspaper ads in large-circulation papers bring immediate responses, and if you're in a hurry to hire they're a good bet. But it's important to write an ad that clearly states your needs; if you're too vague you may be swamped by responses.

A friend of ours placed an ad in the Sunday edition of the *New York Times*. The ad read

WARM LOVING WOMAN TO CARE FOR 8-MONTH-OLD GIRL

LIVE-IN MON.–FRI.

REFERENCES REQ'D.

CALL

She then went away for the weekend.

It wasn't a bad ad, she thought, but when she returned home on Tuesday morning there were 145 messages on her answering machine—and that was before her answering machine ran out of tape!

Where did she go wrong? If our friend had to do it all over again, she would have been more specific. What requirements did she have for the job that were not stated in the ad?

She only wanted someone who was willing to work "on-the-books" (someone willing to report her income to the Internal Revenue Service). She also wanted a person who spoke fluent English; had previous childcare experience; and was willing to shop, do errands, and do light housekeeping.

She was lucky she had a secretary to prescreen the calls for her. Many of us, faced with the same daunting volume of applicants, would spend an entire week on the phone returning calls while wanting nothing more than to crawl into bed and give up. But back to our friend. Of the 145 responses, only 25 were willing to work on-the-books. (Cross off 120 inappropriate applicants.) Of the remaining 25, only 15 met our friend's other requirements (such as English speaking) that she had not considered important enough to state in her ad. How should our friend's ad have read? A few simple changes would have made all the difference.

WARM LOVING WOMAN TO CARE FOR 8-MONTH-OLD GIRL
(not a bad start—it gives specifics of childcare situation; some care givers prefer older children, some prefer boys)

LIVE-IN MON.–FRI.
(good—an important part of job description; it eliminates live-out and part-time applicants, as well as those who don't have a place to go on the weekends)

ON-THE-BOOKS
(or *GREEN CARD REQUIRED*—each states succinctly the employer's requirements of legal immigration status and payment with taxes deducted)

ENGLISH SPEAKING
(five more callers never pick up the phone)

LIGHT HOUSEWORK
(two trained nannies don't bother to call)

EXPERIENCE/REFERENCES REQ'D.
(one recent immigrant and two women who've never worked in the childcare field don't waste their time)

CALL

By clearly stating her actual needs, our friend might have received as many as 90 percent fewer calls (although some people apply even if they're not right for the job); in any case, she would have made her life (and her secretary's) a lot easier. She also would not waste the time of the unqualified job seekers who read the ad.

Ads in smaller papers (or in smaller cities) will of course elicit fewer responses than our friend's ad in the *New York Times,* but if you want the *right* people to respond, it's better to be as precise as possible about your needs. Here are some examples of good newspaper ads.

CHILDCARE/HOUSEKEEPER

NEWTON AREA, SUBURBAN BOSTON. ENGLISH SPEAKING, NONSMOKER, DRIVER'S LICENSE—MATURE, LOVING, AND PATIENT TO CARE FOR THREE BOYS AGED 2, 4, AND 6. SLEEP-IN ONLY. EXP. AND RECENT REFS. REQ'D. WILL SPONSOR. CALL MON.–FRI. 9 A.M.–5 P.M. (PHONE NUMBER).

NANNY

BRITISH TRAINED NANNY (NNEB OR EQUIV.), MANHATTAN. TO CARE FOR GIRLS AGE 3 AND 5. PERM. POSITION. MON.–FRI. LIVE-OUT. PRIOR EXP. AND CHECKABLE REFS. REQ'D. CALL (PHONE NUMBER).

CHILDCARE

LIVE-IN WOMAN EXPERIENCED IN CHILD CARE W/ A DESIRE TO BE PART OF A LOVING FAMILY. MUST LOVE CHILDREN & HAVE ENERGY TO CARE FOR 2 BOYS AGE 2 & 3½. NONSMOKER, LICENSED DRIVER, GREEN CARD. PRIVATE APT. IN BEAUTIFUL HOME, SUBURBAN CONNECTICUT. CALL COLLECT ANYTIME: (PHONE NUMBER).

AU PAIR

GAELIC SPEAKING. NEEDED TO CARE FOR 1½-YR.-OLD GIRL. RELIABLE, ENERGETIC, NONSMOKER. OWN ROOM. CHECKABLE REFS. (PHONE NUMBER).

AU PAIR/CHILDCARE

IMMED. LIVE-IN POS. AVAIL. SUBURB OF PHILADELPHIA FOR YOUNG
WOMAN TO CARE FOR 2 LITTLE GIRLS (3 & 4 YRS. OLD). HOUSEKEEPING,
PVT. RM., NONSMOKER. RESPONSIBLE PERSON, PREFERABLY FRENCH
SPEAKING. DRIVER'S LICENSE A MUST. REFS. CALL 9–5, MON.–FRI.
(PHONE NUMBER).

Should you mention salary in your ad? Some employers state the
salary they are willing to pay, thus eliminating applicants who
require more money. Other employers prefer to negotiate with care
givers in person. You may want to find out what the applicant was
making in her last job before making an offer. But be advised, she is
sure to quickly find out the "going rate" in your neighborhood.

In reality, almost all childcare people ask about salary in their
prescreening telephone interviews. A good rule of thumb is to state
"salary commensurate with qualifications" in your ad. If your best
applicant has fifteen years experience and nothing but raves from
her three former employers, you may be willing to pay her more
than you would pay someone who is less qualified.

Tips for Ad Copy and Placement

Include the following in your ad:

- Type of job (e.g., childcare, childcare and light housekeeping,
  au pair, professional nanny).

- Number, sex, and ages of children.

- Location.

- Hours of work.

- Live-in or live-out.

- Immigration and legal requirements.

- Special conditions (e.g., nonsmoker; pets; own room, bath, television, and telephone; car usage; foreign-language requirements; etc.).

- Phone number to call.

The best day to place your ad in a major metropolitan daily newspaper is generally Sunday, but there are exceptions; you should check with your newspaper's classified ad department to verify. Smaller local weeklies generally have a closing date at least a couple of days before publication.

Employment Agencies

Agencies may claim to be the safest and easiest method of finding household workers, including care givers. The claims, however, are often contradicted by reality.

Before using an agency, it's best to know how they operate. Agencies make their money by charging you and/or your care giver a fee; this may be a flat fee, but it's more likely to be a percentage of the first month or first year's pay. The fee (which could amount to several hundred dollars) is often payable at the time you hire someone. If the care giver doesn't work out within a specified time period, some agencies will give a partial refund and others will try to replace her with another candidate. Because most fees are based on a percentage, agencies try to get their applicants as high a weekly wage as they can. We've found that candidates sent from agencies are often quick to negotiate their salary *down*. Let's face it, they want a job, they know the going rate, and they don't care what the agency is paid.

Many agencies will tell you they check references. Forewarned is forearmed—do not rely on an agency's reference checks. We've discovered that many childcare people use bogus references, and it's unlikely that an agency will do any more than a cursory check, whereas you should be more careful—it's your child. *You should always check references yourself, wherever the care giver applicant comes from and whatever the agency says.*

Do agencies train care givers? Except for those associated with nanny schools or, possibly, baby nurse courses, the answer is generally no. The applicants sent to you may be trained in childcare or not, experienced or not—their most notable qualification may well be that they went to the agency to find work.

Although many parents work with agencies (and, in the words of one mother, find the particular agency they work with "helpful and cooperative"), the chances of finding a perfectly wonderful care giver through an agency are no better than through other, less expensive methods. No household employment agency is completely reliable, and for every good story we've heard about hiring through agencies we've heard a bad one. The most common complaint, one we've heard over and over from parents, is that the agency did not prescreen applicants; that they sent anybody and everybody without regard to the family's stated requirements.

There are, of course, still other ways of finding in-home care givers. Parents from Dallas, for example, told us about finding people by advertising on Spanish-language radio stations; others across the country used parenting centers at their local Ys as resources; still others worked with organizations such as Au Pair in America or professional nanny schools. (For a list of organizations and schools you may be able to use, see appendixes B, C, and D.)

Depending on your timetable you can use any or all of the preceding methods, in whatever combination works best. The only important thing is finding someone—the right someone—to take care of your children.

CHAPTER 4

How to Hire the Right Care Giver

You've thought about your real childcare needs, decided what kind of person you're looking for and determined how to go about finding that person. Now how do you ensure that the one person you finally hire will be right for you and your child?

No one's infallible, but there are ways to improve the odds of finding a care giver who will make you and your child happy and secure. At every step of the hiring process there are objective ways to weed out unacceptable or inappropriate applicants, but in the end, if you're lucky, you are likely to face a choice that's not purely objective—you'll be deciding who's best for your family from among several competent, responsible people.

It's possible that you'll be influenced by some things you don't fully understand; the better you know yourself, the better you'll be able to separate your hidden agenda from your family's real needs. All the experts we've spoken to—psychologists, educators, and doctors, as well as parents and care givers—told us that, in addition to the objective factors, a key part of your decision is bound to be emotional. After interviewing and checking references, after considering and weighing your options, it's your gut feeling that will finally tell you whether the person you hire has the chemistry to fit in with your family. Your child's safety, well-being and happiness (and your peace of mind) are not goals that can be programmed into a home computer. There must be an emotional mesh between the members of your family and your care giver.

EMOTIONAL ISSUES IN HIRING A CARE GIVER

Your relationship with a care giver is, of course, a business relationship between an employer and employee, but it's more than that as well. You're hiring someone to share your child, to love your baby. Although you do yourself and your child a disservice by basing your hiring decision entirely on emotional, subjective factors, many parents and professionals agree that you have to be prepared to let the person you hire enter into the life of your family.

You want her to love your child, to care, to share in your joy when your daughter goes to the potty for the first time or your son takes his first steps and for all the thousands of small, momentous steps in your child's life, you want someone to connect emotionally with you and your child. You want someone who doesn't treat your child as just a job, as just a business relationship.

Of course you may believe that "no one is good enough for my child," but if you do (and it's not unusual), you're setting yourself up for some major problems. Yes, your child is special. But if no one is good enough, then leaving him with someone—anyone—will make you feel as though you're abandoning him, and the guilt you feel is bound to be communicated to him.

Many middle-class and upper-middle-class mothers feel guilty about going back to work and leaving their babies with someone else. Psychiatric professionals assure us this is a normal, healthy attitude, completely consonant with the usual mother-child bonding. At times this separation is made even more poignant by parents' own memories of growing up; a generation ago it was much more usual for a middle-class mother to be at home with her children than in an office. (Parents who grew up as members of the upper classes tend to have much less of a problem with separation, particularly if they themselves had a nanny or a governess. The culture of wealth has for many generations included hiring caretakers to mind the kids. People brought up with hired in-home care as an accepted and usual way of life are not themselves so ambivalent about whether it's the right thing to do for their children.)

Another emotional difficulty many parents face is the conflict between hiring a care giver to become part of the family and maintaining a clear distinction between parent as employer and care giver as employee. Most parents want to hire someone who will love their children and be loved by them in return, yet many are afraid of being replaced in their children's affections (more on this delicate subject later). And as far as your child is concerned you may simply find it hard to be a boss (even if you're in a position of responsibility and authority in your own work). But it's necessary; no matter how much a part of your family your care giver becomes, you are ultimately responsible for your own child's welfare and upbringing.

Try to become aware of the subconscious reasons for hiring a specific person. Does she remind you of someone? Your mother, yourself, an idealized Mary Poppins? Is there something in her manner or background that affects you in a way you don't understand?

One mother we interviewed didn't want to hire anyone like her own mother (a grandmotherly sort); others, feeling a sense of heightened security, are drawn toward such people. Another mother, confronted with a person whose background and personality she perceived to be very much like her own, felt threatened by the idea of coming home and seeing that particular "other" taking care of her child; she decided that she would always be wondering "why not me?"

There may be something in an applicant's background or in the tone of her voice that strikes a chord in you—she may have a plaintive tone that irks you or mannerisms that might remind you of your own childhood with alcoholic parents. Not that the chords struck are always discordant; a person who exudes warmth and confidence, although not necessarily the most objectively qualified applicant, could well be the one who is most capable of giving your child the love and attention he or she needs.

Because the customs and ways of approaching children differ from one culture to another, you may also feel most comfortable hiring someone of your own ethnic background. For example, many Filipino-Americans, Irish-Americans, and people of Japanese or Italian heritage prefer hiring "one of their own" as childcare workers. Whatever your reasons for hiring or not hiring someone, it's important that *you* identify them with sincerity.

THE HIRING PROCESS

You've put an ad in the newspaper (or called an agency, put up bulletin board notices, or sent out word on your personal grape-vine). If you've carefully considered what you're looking for in the way of qualifications for the job, and if you've clearly stated your needs in your ad or notice, you shouldn't be totally deluged with applicants. As you might expect, the largest number of immediate responses will come from a newspaper classified ad.

The *Irish Echo* hit the newsstands this morning. Your phone started ringing even before you finished your first cup of coffee, before you had your school-age child dressed for the school bus. If you own a telephone answering machine, you turned it on; you're letting it do some of your prescreening for you. If not, when you left your house to do your shopping and take the baby to the pediatrician, you assumed that whoever called while you were out would call back. It's now 2:00 P.M.

If you have an answering machine, you check your calls when you return home. You've gotten only thirty-four calls (by tomorrow there'll be sixty). If you don't have a machine, the phone continues ringing—as if you never left. There's no need to be overwhelmed . . . as long as you know what to ask for when you prescreen applicants over the telephone.

PRESCREENING APPLICANTS ON THE TELEPHONE

You can make a preliminary assessment (and weed out a lot of unsatisfactory applicants) on the telephone. A telephone answering machine, used as your first line of communication, is even better— there are some applicants you may be able to disqualify without even having to speak with them.

For example, if you require someone fluent in English and the person couldn't leave a clear, comprehensible message on your answering machine, that may already be enough to cross her off the list. (For further information on hiring non-English-speaking care givers, see this chapter, pages 88–90.)

Also, because it's important that the person you hire is easy to contact in case of an emergency, if she doesn't leave a phone number for you to return her call you may decide not to consider her (even if she calls you back later).

If you're not using an answering machine to screen calls, your current childcare person (if you trust her completely and she's leaving on amicable terms) may do some preliminary screening for you. Or you may ask the secretary in your office to screen your calls.

The first questions to ask an applicant on the phone help you determine whether she's actually applying for the job you outlined in your ad, or whether she's simply calling everyone who advertised in the "Household Help Wanted" section of your newspaper. For example, if your ad read

WARM LOVING WOMAN TO CARE FOR EIGHT-MONTH-OLD GIRL. LIVE-IN MON.–FRI. GREEN CARD REQ'D. ENG. SPEAKING, LIGHT HOUSEWORK. EXP./REFS. REQ'D. CALL.

you could start your telephone interview with questions specific to your ad. "You know the job includes caring for an infant girl and some housework. . . . This is a live-in job, five days a week. . . . It's on-the-books, which means you have to declare your income to the government. . . . Have you done this kind of work before? Can you give me the names and numbers of your references?"

These are all explicit requirements of the job as stated in your ad. If she draws a blank on any of them (and if they really are job requirements), you should thank her, hang up, and move on. Here are some "weeding-out" questions to use in a telephone interview.

On Status

Are you willing to work on-the-books/off-the-books?

When you come for your interview, can you show me your social security card/green card?

On Hours/General Job Requirements

This is a live-in job.

We want you to work forty-five hours a week, Monday through Friday.

The job includes light housework.

And, for all of the above: Are you still interested?

Do you smoke?

Do you like pets?

Do you have a driver's license?

Specific to Childcare

Do you have experience in taking care of children?

Have you worked for another family previously?

How old were the children?

Why did you leave?

What salary did you make in your last job?

Why do you like working with children?

What kinds of things do you like to do with them?

I'd like to check your references before you come in for an interview. (It's a good idea to try to get references at this stage; if a person is serious—and truthful—she should be willing to give you names and numbers now. If she isn't willing, she should have a reason.)

Here are some examples of other things to watch out for (and find out more about) in your preliminary telephone screening. If she says she watched school-age kids, ask her what school they attended. If she says she doesn't remember, or something along the lines of, "Oh, just the school down the street," she could be lying.

If you care about age, personal appearance, and habits, you may ask the applicant to describe herself. (This is easier than you may think. One parent we interviewed found that all but one of twenty-odd applicants, when asked to describe themselves, gave a physical description first.)

If you're concerned about physical condition and energy level, you may be able to find out more if you tell her, for example, that every day your older child goes to a class that's a thirty-block, round-trip walk; would she be willing to walk the baby in the stroller to class every day?

It's also helpful to listen carefully to the questions the applicant asks you. It will help you get a better sense of the person, of her motivations and experience, and it will also help you decide whether you want to consider her for the job of taking care of your children. (If all she wants to talk about are working conditions, salary, hours, vacations, sick days, etc., and shows no interest in your family or your children, she may be better suited for another kind of job.)

You may want to add other questions—or go in other directions entirely—depending on what's most important to you. Just remember, if you think about what you want to know before you pick up the phone you'll save a lot of time and energy in the long run.

By asking the right questions on the phone, listening carefully to the responses, and calling the references of those you wish to consider further, you will probably have narrowed the field considerably. How do you evaluate those who are left—the ones who've successfully passed through your preliminary screening?

THE INTERVIEW

Before hiring someone, a face-to-face interview is essential—no matter how impressed you might have been from speaking with her on the telephone and regardless of the raves she may have gotten from references. A personal interview is about asking questions, finding out information, probing for personality traits and job experience, and seeing if there is any chemistry between you and the applicant.

Letting Your Child Help You Decide

If it's at all possible, let your children help you make the choice. Both parents and professionals agree that seeing the applicant with your child helps you as much, if not more, than any questions you could conceive of asking her.

Of course, if you've decided to interview a dozen people, this may be a strain on your child. It is unfair to a child to ask her to choose between—or even to relate to—so many strangers. A better way might be to plan on a two-interview hiring process: the first with just adults (yourselves and the applicant) and the second, for the few applicants you are still considering, with your child present as well. (See pages 86–87 for more about how many interviews to schedule.) That way you can see the interaction between the applicant and your child (and with a verbal child hear her opinions) without putting undue stress on your child.

Developmental psychologist Dr. Irving Sigel believes it's best to have your child present from the very beginning of the interview, that you should introduce your child to the prospective care giver at the same time you introduce yourself. Although it's a job interview (and therefore necessarily somewhat strained and formal), Dr. Sigel suggests you observe how the person greets your child, whether she talks to him and seems comfortable.

Childbirth educator Charlene Stokamer told us that, in interviewing someone to care for a baby, essentially what you're looking for is whether she acts in a motherly way: Is there eye contact between the care giver and the baby, does the applicant croon and rock the baby, and is she warm and loving?

One mother told us that several people she interviewed marveled at the view in her Chicago lakefront apartment while barely noticing her baby. The person she eventually hired headed straight for the baby, made immediate eye contact and asked to hold her during the course of the interview.

Some people come into interviews and never ask to see the child at all. No matter how otherwise competent she may appear, we believe it's best to beware of someone who acts in this way; the most important qualification for this job is how well the applicant relates to some of the most important people in your life—your children.

Letting your child help you make the choice is relatively simple in the case of an infant; you're mostly looking for the care giver's warmth and ability to be loving and whether your baby responds. With older children it's a little more complicated.

First and foremost, you have to know your own children; you can't expect your children's personalities or moods to be miraculously transformed simply on the approach of a new person. Your children's ages and personalities, as well as factors as basic as fatigue and hunger, play a large role in determining their initial responses to a potential care giver. Your child may not react well to strangers; why should it be different with this particular stranger? Your child may be angry because he loved a previous childcare person and doesn't want her replaced. Or he may feel that if it weren't for this person his mom would stay home and take care of him. An older child may try to dominate the interview, or he may try to get away with behavior he would never try with you. From a very early age, children learn that there are different sets of rules and ways to behave with different people.

You'll want to determine whether there can be communication and mutual respect between your child and the care giver. You may be concerned about whether an applicant can deal with your children's sibling rivalry; whether she can deal with playmates in a way you feel comfortable about; whether she will enforce discipline in a way that's consistent with your desires; whether she's playful, friendly, and spontaneous; and whether she can support your child educationally (help with homework, show interest in accomplishments, etc.). You might get more accurate answers to these questions by observing the interaction between your child and the applicant than by a dozen direct questions in the absence of your child. If you need to discuss something away from your child, Dr. Sigel suggests that you do it at another meeting or have someone else present to be with the child for a few minutes while the interview continues.

If your three- or four-year-old acts up during the interview, Dr. Sigel believes there are two basic principles to follow: Don't embarrass your child and don't reprimand him in front of the applicant. Take your child into another room and talk with him about the situation; reassure him (he might be afraid you're going to leave him with the sitter that day), and after he's calmed down bring him back into the process. (If you've told your child beforehand that someone was coming and why, some of your child's anxiety and acting-out problems may be prevented.)

Before Questions and Answers

Help make the applicant (and yourself) feel comfortable. Relax, offer her coffee or a glass of water, offer her a seat. She will act more like herself if she feels welcome.

In any interview situation, the person being interviewed is trying to impress the interviewer. As Elaine Ruskin of the Family Center at New York's West Side Y told us, "When a person comes for an interview in your home she's at her best. So if you don't like her, it's only going to go downhill." Ms. Ruskin believes it's most important to spend time with an applicant and have her spend time with your child, even if that means paying her on an hourly basis (as if coming to baby-sit) for a second interview, before you hire her. And, she cautions, although the questions you ask are important, questions themselves, no matter how probing and pertinent they may be, will not give you the whole picture. Indeed, some applicants may be nervous and inarticulate in a question-and-answer interview session, but warm, playful, and loving when given a chance to interact with you and your children in a less-structured setting.

Questions and Answers

The following questions are all pertinent to an in-home care giver's employment interview.* They are not exhaustive of everything you might ask; depending on your situation you may have other specific questions in mind. Also, the answer you get to any one question may lead you into an entirely new line of thought. We urge you to ask only those questions you must have answered and to be flexible enough to modify questions, move in different directions, and develop your own interview technique.

If you were to ask every question here in the order they appear, you would probably know quite a bit about the applicant, but it could also take a lot more of your time than you're willing to spend and it would be a less personal interview. So pick and choose carefully, and find out what you need to know.

There are no right and wrong answers to many of these questions; it's more a matter of your own judgment about what suits your family. And it's not a graded exam; someone may be right for the job even though she gives some "wrong" answers. As child psychiatrist Dr. William Koch, founder and director of the Skhool for Parents (that's right, Skhool), told us, "You can't base your whole reason for hiring or not hiring on the basis of one answer. More to the point is that a person expresses a willingness to learn."

---

* You may notice that some of these questions are the same as those listed for hiring a baby nurse. The answers to these questions may be important to you no matter what kind of childcare worker you hire.

100 Questions (More or Less) to Ask in an Interview (and What to Look For in the Answers)

After introducing yourselves and getting settled, the first thing you should do in an interview is set a tone that will allow you to get as much information as possible. Put the person at ease, make yourself comfortable, and begin.

Start by finding out a little about her background, but don't approach her with a barrage of questions. Allow her to express herself without feeling as though she's on trial.

Background Questions

Have you worked with kids before? What were their ages?

What age children do you like best and why?

How long have you been doing this kind of work?

What did you like about your last job?

What didn't you like about it?

Why did you leave your last job?

Why do you do this work? Do you find it rewarding?

What's in this job for you?

Do you have children of your own? Any younger brothers or sisters you helped raise? Tell me about them. (Fretta Reitzes, director of the Parenting Center at New York's 92nd Street Y, says, "You want to deflect the interview from a straight question/answer situation. Ask about her family. Ask about her hometown or native country.)

After settling down, it might be time to continue with some questions about attitudes. Because you want to hire someone whose actions will be consistent with your own, it's important for you to try to determine whether her cultural biases will prevent that. Whether determined by culture or personality, attitudes on discipline, childhood sexuality, religion, and other matters are key to determining whether a care giver can mesh with your family.

Sex and Sexuality

What do you think about boys? Girls?

What would you do if you saw a little boy playing with his sister's dolls? A little girl playing with her brother's trucks? (A parent's orientation may be to discourage sexual stereotyping but child-care workers, particularly those with less education, may believe this kind of play will lead to homosexuality—Dr. Irving Sigel.)

What would you do if you saw a child playing with himself or herself?

What would you do if you saw children involved in sex play at the age of three or four? (Dr. Sigel believes very strongly that the parents are responsible for a child's attitudes on sexuality; he feels a care giver should calmly break up a situation involving children's sex play by diverting the children's attention, then tell parents what happened. The parents should decide what is acceptable. If a childcare person tells a child, "Don't touch yourself there," while the parents think it's okay, the child will get a mixed, and very confusing message.)

Conflict and Discipline

What kinds of problems have you had with kids?

What would you do if the child is in his room playing by himself?

What if the child won't eat?

What do you do if he throws his plate on the floor?

What if she won't take a nap?

What if he disobeys when you want him to do something? When you tell him to stop doing something dangerous?

What would you do if the child you're watching has a fight with another child in the playground?

How do you handle fighting between brothers and sisters?

What if a child comes home crying from a fight at a next door neighbor's?

How do you handle tantrums?

What if the child says something derogatory to you?

What would you say if the child bit you or hit you?

What do you do when you become angry at a child?

How do you discipline children?

Different cultures have varying attitudes on discipline. For example, some cultures believe spanking is acceptable punishment while others do not. Dr. William Koch says that parents and childcare people should have the same disciplinary attitude. Other child development experts, including Dr. Sigel, told us that whatever the difference in attitude, the single most important factor regarding a care giver and discipline is that she carry out your wishes without hesitation or ambivalence. The prime responsibility for discipline is with the parent; the childcare worker just executes.

If you are seriously concerned about cultural compatibility, you may be able to find out more about her cultural biases with just a little bit of digging. For example, some people may find even

common bedtime prayers (e.g., ". . . if I die before I wake . . .")
problematic, objecting to them either on principle or because they
are troubled by specific emotional implications. If you have these
concerns, ask an applicant if she ever put the child to bed, and if the
bedtime ritual included prayer. (If it did, ask her if the parents
wanted the child to pray and how she felt about it.) You may ask her
if she attends church; her attitude toward religion in general may
influence your decision. And if, for example, you're a devout Catho-
lic and she's a member of an evangelical denomination that stresses
conversion, you may not want her to be a principal care giver to your
children. There is nothing wrong with preferring someone whose
cultural background is compatible with your own. Indeed, one of
the most important aspects of hiring a care giver is finding someone
you feel comfortable and secure with.

Of course, it's possible to find someone who comes from a different cultural milieu but who shares your basic value system. A
person who's honest and forthright, warm and caring, hard working and self-motivated, or intuitive and sensitive can come from any
background—from the Philippines to Philadelphia.

The questions you ask about duties, job philosophy, and job
competence will to a large extent be contingent on the ages of your
children and where you live. For example, a two-year-old needs to
play with other children and be stimulated to learn while an infant's
needs are for basic care and nurturing. In addition, you are design-
ing a job that depends on your own individual needs. For example,
if you live in the suburbs you will most likely need someone who
drives; if your child is in school part-time you may want someone to
combine childcare and housework.

Job Demands and Philosophy—Baby

How do you handle the baby's feeding schedule?

What kind of diapers do you like?

When you change a baby, do you use lotion? Powder? Anything?

Will you give the baby a bath?

Do you always sterilize baby bottles or can you use a dishwasher?

How do you get a baby to behave? (Most child development experts believe that an infant cries only out of physical need, including nurturing—in other words, a baby cannot misbehave—and the question is, therefore, a leading one.)

When do you use a pacifier?

Should a baby be picked up as soon as he cries, or should he cry it out?

Do you think a baby should see other babies?

Job Demands and Philosophy—Toddlers and Older Children

How do you feel about setting up play dates for the child with other children?

Will you take him to, and participate in, his art/gym/music class?

Will you pick him up at school?

How do you deal with two children who are fighting over the same toy?

Do you read to children?

Do you play games with them?

Do you think of yourself as a teacher?

What do you consider to be your responsibilities in this job?

How do you feel about combining housework and childcare?

How old do you think a child should be when he or she is toilet trained? Have you ever been involved with toilet training a child? What did you do?

Did you ever try to get a child off a bottle? At what age do you think that's appropriate? How did it go?

How much television do you think a child should watch? Which shows?

Situational Responses

What do you do when a baby has gas? A fever?

What about a medical emergency? Do you know CPR?

What do you do for a baby who cries all the time? A baby who won't sleep? A colicky baby?

What would you do if a child choked on a piece of food?

At what point would you call us at work?

At what point would you call a pediatrician?

Job Demands—Household

Do you drive? Do you have a valid driver's license? Will you be able to drive the children? Have you ever been in an automobile accident? Can you tell me about it?

Do you like dogs/cats? Will you walk the dog? Change the cat's litter? Feed the animals?

Do you cook? How do you feel about cooking for the children/ family?

(Live-out) How will you get to and from work? If we come home late or need you to baby-sit after your regular hours, what is your availability?

(Live-in) What time are you ready to start in the morning? What would you do if the children knocked on your door on your day off? Can we call on you to work late hours occasionally?

In addition to all the preceding questions, it makes sense to ask questions that directly concern her compatibility with your household situation; these questions range from her personal habits to her feelings about your work and marital status.

Household Compatibility and Personal Information

How do you feel about working for a mother who works part-time/full-time/not at all?

Have you ever worked for a family where the father was actively involved with his children on a day-to-day basis? How do you feel about working for that kind of father?

Have you ever worked for a single parent? Do you have any feelings about working for a single parent?

Do you know the neighborhood? Do you know any other child-care people in this area?

Do you smoke? How do you feel about our smoking?

(Live-in) Do you like to go out or stay in your room at night or on your days off?

Do you have a social security card and a green card and/or proof of citizenship? (This documentation is required for hiring someone on-the-books.)

What are your favorite television shows? (If she mentions soap operas and you forbid television during the day, beware.)

Do you have any physical problems or conditions that we should know about? Is there anything that might affect your work? What medications are you taking? (These questions should be phrased in a nonthreatening manner. For example, if you do not believe that a diabetic condition or hypertension automatically disqualifies a prospective care giver from employment, you should not make her feel as though it does. This is not to say that you should not know about these types of condition, on the contrary, they are things that you should know about—as much for the care giver's well-being as for your children's.)

Will you agree to a physical? (With the increased concern throughout society about acquired immunodeficiency syndrome [AIDS] and drug abuse, more and more families are asking prospective childcare employees this question—and demanding a statement of health.)

There are a lot of other questions that you would like to ask, but can't. For example, if a person has a history of drug or alcohol abuse or mental illness, has been convicted of a crime, or has been fired with cause from a previous childcare job, she's unlikely to tell you; the best you can do is try to find these things out indirectly. If you have any questions concerning these matters at the end of an interview, there's clearly something wrong and you should eliminate the applicant from consideration. (Of course, if a person volunteers the information that she was treated for depression ten years earlier, but has not had a recurrence, you might well have a different approach, making your decision rest on your own ability to deal with her past, and possibly taking into consideration her honesty in bringing up the matter.)

What you need to find out in order to feel comfortable about hiring someone is up to you. You can ask all the above questions and a hundred others, but more important than any question is how attuned you are to the person in front of you. What is she like? How does she respond to your child and how does your child respond to her? How does she make you feel? Can you communicate? Do you think she can provide your child with the warmth, understanding, and security he or she needs. What kind of personality does the applicant have? Is she happy? Is she playful? Does she have a sense of humor? Is she reassuring and warm? Is she mature? Is she giving? Is she responsible?

If you don't feel comfortable with a person, you can cut off the interview anytime you want. If you do feel comfortable, you can talk more about specific job requirements, or you can have a more candid (and less formal) discussion about your respective views on child rearing.

SAMPLE INTERVIEWS

No two interviews are alike. And although interviews do not reveal everything about a job applicant, they certainly help. You form your impressions in many ways, the least important of which may be the specific answers given by the prospective care giver to your questions. Following are two fictitious interview situations. In each case, the individuals are based on composites of applicants interviewed by ourselves or by other parents who spoke with us about their experiences.

Situation 1

The living room of a typical middle-class, urban family. The doorbell rings and a mother and her two-year-old daughter go to the intercom.

DOORMAN (*through the intercom*): A Mrs. Johnson is at the door.

MOTHER: Send her up. (*to her daughter*) Jane Johnson is coming. Remember, Mommy told you we're going to talk to her for a while to see if we want her to help take care of us.

DAUGHTER: Daddy too?

MOTHER: Yes, Daddy too.
(At that moment, the doorbell rings. Mother and daughter answer the door.)

DAUGHTER: I want to get it.
(Daughter opens the door. Jane Johnson is at the door. She's a slightly overweight, almost middle-aged woman. She's dressed neatly and simply, in bright colors.)

DAUGHTER: What's your name?
(Jane Johnson leans down in order to speak to the little girl.)

JANE JOHNSON: My name is Jane. What's your name?
(Daughter runs away giggling.)

MOTHER: Hello, I'm Maggie Jones. Come on in, take off your coat and make yourself at home.
(Jane Johnson takes off her coat and shoes.)

JANE JOHNSON: I never walk on the carpets with my shoes.

MOTHER: Please sit down.
(Maggie sits down and her daughter snuggles beside her.)

JANE JOHNSON: How old are you, sweetheart?
(The little girl hides behind her mother.)

JANE JOHNSON: I bet you're two years old.

MOTHER: How did you hear about this agency?
(Jane is playing peek-a-boo with the little girl.)

JANE JOHNSON: (*to the mother*) A friend of mine got a job through them.

(*to the daughter*) I took care of a little boy who was just about your age. (The daughter smiles.)

JANE JOHNSON: (*to both*) He was such a sweet boy, except he wouldn't take his nap.

MOTHER: I would prefer that Jennifer not take naps.

JANE JOHNSON: Oh. (*pause*) I understand what you mean. It depends on the child, I suppose. The last family I worked for, the Michaels, felt the same way. Once he was two, Leonard couldn't fall asleep at night if he slept during the day. When Leonard looked like he was getting tired . . . (*She laughs.*) Oh, some of the things I had to do to keep that boy awake. But some little children need their sleep.

MOTHER: What do you think?
(Jane Johnson laughs.)

JANE JOHNSON: Everybody's different. You can't treat every child the same way.

MOTHER: How long did you work for the . . . Michaels?

JANE JOHNSON: Two and a half years. It was nice . . . I had a friend from my country who worked for their neighbors. That's how I got the job. It was nice . . . sometimes the children played together and, y'know, stuff like that. They're good people.

MOTHER: Why don't you work for them anymore?

DAUGHTER: Mommy?

MOTHER: I'm talking to Jane now, sweetheart.

JANE JOHNSON: It's okay. Come here, honey, and let me see how big you are. (The daughter walks over to Jane proudly and stands as tall as she can.)

JANE JOHNSON: Oh, you are a big little girl.
(She holds out her arms to the daughter inviting her to come up on her lap. The daughter jumps up.)

JANE JOHNSON: (*to the mother*) I'm sorry, what was that question again?

MOTHER: Why did you leave your last job?

JANE JOHNSON: Mr. Michael's company transferred him to Boston. Here, I have a reference from Mrs. Michael right here. (*She starts looking in her pocketbook.*) Somewhere.
(Should the interview continue?)

Situation 2

The living room of a typical middle-class, urban family. The door-bell rings and a woman goes to answer it. The sounds of "Sesame Street" come from the bedroom. The woman opens the door and sees JANE JOHNSON. Jane is an attractive woman, about thirty years old, dressed in "interview clothes"—a conservative suit with a straight skirt and high heels.

MOTHER: Hello, I'm Maggie Jones.

JANE JOHNSON: I'm Jane Johnson.
(She walks past Maggie into the room and looks around.)

JANE JOHNSON: Is that "Sesame Street"?

MOTHER: Yes.

JANE JOHNSON: Very nice. (*She looks around.*) You have a lovely apartment, Mrs. Jones. (*She looks out the window.*) Very nice.

MOTHER: Won't you sit down.
(Jane sits in an armchair and the mother sits in a chair opposite her.)

MOTHER: The agency said you're planning to leave your present job.

JANE JOHNSON: That's right.

MOTHER: Have you been there long?

JANE JOHNSON: A long time. More than a year.

MOTHER: Can you tell me why you're planning to leave?

JANE JOHNSON: I don't like it.

MOTHER: Uh huh.

JANE JOHNSON: First of all, they don't pay me enough. I need seven fifty an hour.

MOTHER: Uh huh.

JANE JOHNSON: You'll pay seven fifty an hour?

MOTHER: It's possible. What did you do in the job?

JANE JOHNSON: I took care of the kids. Y'know, I picked them up at school, I fed them dinner, I played with them, gave them a bath, stuff like that. I don't like to do heavy housework. That was another one of the problems. It's too much when you gotta take care of kids, don't you think? (*She looks out the window.*) You have a wonderful view.

MOTHER: I would like you to do some straightening up, washing dishes, making the beds . . .

JANE JOHNSON: Yours too?

MOTHER: Yeah.
(Jane raises her eyebrows.)

MOTHER: I have some sort of general questions to ask you, if it's okay. About your style of . . . about your philosophy, how you think kids should be taken care of. For example, I'm very concerned about discipline. Do you have any thoughts about discipline?

JANE JOHNSON: Sure. I think discipline is very important.

MOTHER: You do?

JANE JOHNSON: Absolutely.

MOTHER: How do you think a child should be disciplined?

JANE JOHNSON: That depends on the situation. What do you think?
(Should the interview continue?)

In analyzing these interviews, would you consider hiring either Jane Johnson? What would be your evaluation of each of them? Would you conduct an interview the way either Maggie does? Here's what we think.

The first Jane Johnson was a bit of a scatterbrain. However, from the very beginning of the interview, when she took off her shoes on entering (an act that might be thought of as anything from respectful to flaky), she was spontaneous, often to the detriment of the "impression" she might make.

Jane number 1 was dressed in a very natural, clearly personal style. At times she didn't follow the mother's line of questioning and she either forgot to bring her reference letter or never had one to begin with. (What do you think? Did she forget it? If she left it at home, would you ask her to send it to you, or would you just ask her to give you the reference's phone number to follow up.)

Jane number 1 was also easily flustered in dealing with Maggie. When the talk came to the question of naps, this Jane had to backtrack to explain herself; her immediate response was somewhat confused (she may have been trying to impress and felt she slipped up), but we think that in the end she summed up her basic philosophy of child rearing in one simple statement: "Everybody's different. You can't treat every child the same way."

This Jane surely wasn't on top of all her answers. But she was extremely attentive to the little girl, and her attentiveness was reciprocated.

As for the mother, Maggie number 1 wasn't totally in control of this situation; her daughter and Jane set much of the tone for the interview with their interaction. But this Maggie was also nonjudgmental in the manner of her questioning; she was able to elicit certain essentially honest responses and thus may have been able to ascertain in a very short time Jane's lack of rigidity (or organization). She may have been frustrated when, at times, Jane became distracted and didn't answer her questions directly, but on the other hand, she might have found Jane's personal warmth and obvious rapport with children a big plus.

Jane Johnson number 2 seized control of the terms of the interview almost from the start; the conversation focused around her concerns and not the mother's. She was clearly intelligent, articulate, and sure of herself; whether these traits would necessarily translate into being a great care giver for a two-year-old is somewhat problematic.

This Jane complimented Maggie on her home in an attempt to ingratiate herself. She was far from candid in her direct responses to Maggie's questions, instead turning the answers around so that her own concerns—about pay, job duties, etc.—remained more prominent than Maggie's concerns. In addition, she never asked about the child she was supposed to take care of, and after all, isn't that what the job is about?

Just as Jane number 2 took control of the interview, Maggie number 2 lost control. She was a little defensive with Jane and backed off from pursuing those things that were most important to her. She finally reached the point of asking Jane's permission to ask questions, thus leaving the way open for Jane to continue to answer only those questions she wanted to. Indeed, Maggie was unable to get a direct, clear response from Jane about her feelings about discipline (something that Maggie stated was very important to her).

Jane number 2's response to the question about discipline, "That depends on the situation," is a very different statement from Jane number 1's, "Everybody's different. You can't treat every child the same way." It's clear from the context that Jane number 2 was trying to determine Maggie's feelings before committing herself, but Jane number 1 seemed completely sincere in her answer, even though the answer was preceded by an inarticulate, confused attempt to say the right thing.

HOW MANY INTERVIEWS?

If you like someone, but aren't quite sure whether to hire her, the ideal solution is to have her come back for a second interview. (Some people feel it's essential to have a care giver come for two interviews—the first with parents only, the second with parents and children.) In addition to your children, you might want other family members to meet her and help you decide, or you may simply want to delve deeper into one or another aspect of the job requirements.

If you do call somebody back for a second interview, it makes sense to have her spend an hour or so with your child in a relatively unsupervised setting. You may wander in and out of the room and observe their interaction, or watch how they get along when they're together in your neighborhood playground, but essentially this is a "play" interview, one in which your child gets a first impression of a care giver on his own turf.

We know of families who've called people back for several interviews. This may help assure you that you're making the right decision, but it could well be seen by the childcare applicant as an imposition (it does cost her time and money). So if you do call someone back for a second or third interview, a good faith gesture on your part might be to reimburse her for her expenses and pay her for her time. Dr. Elaine Ruskin believes the best policy after the first interview is to pay an applicant the same hourly rate as she would get if she were working for you.

Don't rush into a decision you're not completely comfortable with. But remember, somebody who's really good might be snapped up by someone else while you're straddling the fence.

People who have previously hired in-home childcare workers often have a more specific job description in mind than those who are hiring for the first time. These experienced childcare employers may, therefore, be more decisive, finding it easier to interview and easier to make a decision than families hiring care givers for the first time.

And there are emotional issues involved in your hiring decisions as well: Fence-sitting might be, particularly if it's the first time you've ever left your child with someone other than a family member, an expression of your own emotional state. (Of course, fence-sitting may also suggest your ambivalence about hiring a particular person.)

The Other Side of the Interview

An interview is a two-way street; care givers interview you at the same time you're interviewing them. A really good childcare person is someone who's in great demand; she may well be in a position to decide for herself which of several jobs she wants to take. The decision about who you're going to hire, therefore, is not entirely up to you. (Care givers, like other workers, appreciate being told where they stand. Tell an applicant how many people you're interviewing for the job, when you will make your decision, and when you'll call her back.)

We're not saying that you should be anything other than yourselves at the interview; trying to impress a prospective employee (even if she will be taking care of your children) is not the point. What you want to learn—and presumably what she wants to know as well—is whether she and your family are compatible and comfortable with each other.

A number of care givers we spoke with told us they turned down jobs because they felt the family wasn't neat enough. What this meant to them was that it would be their job to get the house in order, and that wasn't what they wanted to do (nor ostensibly was it what they were being hired to do). But you don't have to shampoo the rugs before interviewing anyone; you should present yourselves, your home, and your family as you really are. (If you pretend to be someone you're not, eventually the person you hire will find out anyway. She's not required to stay with you if she feels that you've misrepresented yourselves, and she's perfectly within her rights to leave if she's unhappy.)

Here's a list of some of the particulars care givers told us they want to know.

- Salary and benefits

- Hours

- Duties

- Expected daily schedule (will she take child to school in morning, bathe children before dinner, etc.)

- How much decision making is expected of her as regards both children and household

- What type of discipline is expected and how much say she'll have in it

It's best to be prepared to discuss all these matters and others that may be of concern to prospective employees at the time of the interview.

HIRING SOMEONE WHO DOESN'T SPEAK ENGLISH

Hiring a care giver who doesn't speak English may appear to have its benefits. We know of one Los Angeles family who hired a Spanish-speaking childcare worker who spoke no English because they felt it preserved their privacy (they assumed she didn't understand what they said to each other); a couple in Dallas hired a person who knew no English because she would be less likely to be independent, and less likely to leave as long as they wanted to continue employing her; others have told us they feel they can pay a non-English-speaking childcare worker less than the going rate for someone fluent in English. We don't think these are positive reasons for hiring someone; we feel that they are not only lacking in respect of the care giver's needs as a human being but they also don't serve your children's needs for nurturing and understanding.

Most of the authorities we consulted feel the negatives of hiring someone lacking fluency in English far outweigh the positives. Fretta Reitzes, director of the Parenting Center at New York's 92nd Street Y, was emphatic, "Because of safety issues, I can't understand why anyone would hire someone who speaks no English. When you think of all the things that may not be right with your childcare person, the language barrier just adds to it."

If you don't speak her language, there's a further question: How can you communicate with a person you can't talk to? How can you find out what's happening with your child in your absence. But even if *you* can communicate with her, you are running another risk—how can someone who is noncommunicative in English respond in case of an emergency? Someone who is borderline conversant in English will even have problems in everyday play situations such as intervening in an argument between two kids, or in helping your child develop language skills.

If your care giver can't communicate with you, think about the effect of a language barrier on your children. If the care giver can't talk to your child or understand what he is saying, then you are doing your child a real disservice.

If your care giver has some knowledge of English, you may think—and be absolutely correct in thinking—that her skills will increase. She may well have other qualities that outweigh her weak language skills.

You have to decide for yourselves how much English is necessary. If you're going to hire someone who can't speak English fluently you have to find out, to your own satisfaction, how she is going to handle the problematic situations that are bound to arise from lack of English-language skills.

HIRING A CARE GIVER WHO SPEAKS A FOREIGN LANGUAGE

If your idea is that your child will become bilingual because he has a French-speaking nanny, then you may be proceeding on a thread-bare assumption—that your current childcare person will be with you forever. That's an exceedingly rare occurence; the likelihood of true permanence is minimal.

If you yourselves are immigrants or bilingual, you may want to hire someone who speaks your other language. That's a fine idea, but adding a second language to the necessary qualifications makes it that much more difficult to find a good care giver who meets your other needs. Of course, it's not impossible, particularly in a large metropolitan area such as New York or in a region with many people who speak the same language you do. You may, however, expect to pay a premium if you have a dual-language requirement.

CHECKING REFERENCES

Here are a couple of true stories that will show just how important it is to check references.

A professional couple in New York City hired a young woman without a reference check; the woman soon disappeared with $10,000 worth of jewelry. The couple checked references after the fact; they heard similar stories from all the people they called. They then telephoned the girl's parents, who told them that their daughter was a drug addict.

Maybe the employers should have recognized something strange in the young woman's behavior from her interview, but they didn't. That's not unusual. Sometimes people are able to hide personality flaws, drug and alcohol abuse, and antisocial behavior in an interview situation, or even in the short period of intense scrutiny after they're hired for a job. But what these parents should have done, and it wouldn't have taken too much effort, was to simply pick up the phone before they hired this young woman. It would have saved them a lot of money, and spared them a lot of grief. And these people were lucky—their loss was only money.

Another couple hired a care giver who subsequently worked for them for nine months. When they hired her, they checked her references, but in a cursory manner, only listening to what they wanted to hear. They didn't check her passport or other photo identification; they didn't ask the references for a physical description; they didn't ascertain without a doubt that the person was who she said she was. In fact it turned out she was using an assumed name (having stolen someone else's identification and references), and in the end it became apparent that she was planning to abduct the child, having systematically removed all pictures and other means of identifying the child from the home. In this case, the parents discovered what was happening just in time to prevent a tragedy.

Granted, these are extreme examples; it's unlikely that anything so upsetting or horrifying would ever happen to you. But each story shows the absolute necessity of checking references—and checking carefully. In checking references, a basic rule is the more questions you ask, the more information you'll get. You'll want to assure yourself that the person being talked about is indeed the person you yourself met. You'll want to learn more about who she is, how she responds to different situations, how loving and caring and responsible she is. You can't ask every question, but you can assess a person's truthfulness about her past, as well as get a sense of what to expect from her in the future.

When speaking to a reference, it's important to determine who you're talking to. It should be relatively easy to tell whether a reference is bogus (relatives and friends have been known to lie for applicants, and a little probing can determine if a relationship is indeed one of employer and employee). If the person you're speaking to is legitimate, it is possible that her philosophy of child rearing and view of life is entirely different from your own—and those differences could have a large bearing on what you hear from her as well as on what you may expect from the care giver. Try to assess what that particular employer expected from the worker, and what she got. Then apply her experience to your own situation.

Listen carefully to the person you're speaking with. Listen for changes in tone of voice, to guarded responses, to which questions a reference is reluctant to answer. Beware of answers such as, "She did the cleaning, but . . . ," or "She was good for one of her kind." Hear what's really being said—ask, "but what?" and "exactly what 'kind' was she?" When speaking to references, ask questions that are simple and direct, but also ask some that are indirect and probe beneath the surface. Find out what you have to find out. Following are some questions you might want to ask a reference.

What were her dates of employment? Her hours?

What did you pay her?

Was there any other compensation I should know about?

How old were your kids when she worked for you?

What were her duties? Describe her day? (You can hear what's really being said if their words are something like, "She was supposed to come at eight but she was always late.")

How many sick days did she take?

Did you ever see any problem with alcohol or drug use?

Was she homesick? (This question is for au pairs, immigrant workers, and people who recently moved from other cities or areas.)

How much housework did she do? Did you have other household help?

Did she ever have to respond to an emergency situation? What did she do?

Did you let her discipline your children? How did she handle it? How did she handle your children when they had tantrums?

What did your kids call her?

What did she do with the children on a rainy day?

Did she watch television during her work time? How much television did the children watch when she worked for you?

Did you organize your child's activities? How much initiative did she take? (These kinds of questions tell you as much about the reference as it does about the applicant.)

Did you ever change the "contract" of your relationship by adding new responsibilities, etc? If you asked her to do more work, what was her response?

Did she eat with the family?

Does she have any family that you know of?

Did her family life or religion affect your relationship with her in any way?

What did she do on her time off? How did she relate to the children on her time off? (For live-in workers.)

Why do you think she does this kind of work?

Why isn't she with you anymore? Would you hire her again if she came to you now?

If you have a new person, can you describe her to me? How is she different from the person applying for the job in our home?

Were you home a lot when she worked for you, or were you out of the house most of the time?

People are very reluctant to give bad references; they're more likely to withhold in their responses rather than say anything negative about the person. For example, one working mother in New Jersey told us, "This woman grew up in foster care. Her former boyfriend called and bothered her. One night when she was alone with the kids he threw rocks through the windows of our house. He was jailed for one month, so we gave her a month to find a new job. I told her I'd give her a good reference because her work was fine, but I suggested that she might not want to live in somebody else's home."

Other parents tell similar stories. They don't necessarily mean to be dishonest, but their sense of responsibility to their former employee often leads to omissions that can be crucial to your decision. It's up to you to get beyond the omissions and determine the truth.

YOU'VE DECIDED TO HIRE SOMEONE

You've made a decision; after all the phone calls, interviews, and reference checking you finally know who you want to hire. Now it's time to speak with your prospective care giver more specifically than ever before about your needs and in so doing to come to an agreement about wages, hours, duties, etc.

Some people find it necessary to put the terms of this agreement in writing as a letter to the employee. They believe it creates less of a chance for misunderstanding, because it clarifies the rights and responsibilities of both employer and employee, and that it puts the relationship on a more professional level.

But as with most childcare questions, there are wide differences of opinion on this subject. Many parents feel that a written agreement with a care giver is a formality at best and a daunting and off-putting proposition at worst. They contend that it limits options, that it sets up a relationship that can't change with changing needs, and that rather than building trust, it breeds mistrust.

These people opt for greater spontaneity, for having the ability to change the terms of the agreement when necessary. If you choose to have this type of flexible agreement, then you must be very confident that your care giver is trustworthy and that a strong rapport will develop between you. And you must be ready to discuss, explain, and negotiate. Even if you feel you need a high level of informality and flexibility, you also need some structure—it's important to be very clear at the outset and at any time that your requirements change about exactly what your expectations are. You may talk about what you want from your care giver before she starts working, and during the period immediately following, you may discuss and adjust your requirements and expectations frequently. But you must be clear and reasonable.

If you decide to put your agreement in writing, it's best to make it as general as possible, and not as specific as, "You are responsible for making and giving Billy lunch every Monday, Tuesday, and Wednesday; you are to change Jenny's bedding twice a week; you are to make play dates every Monday afternoon." Yes, you can be specific about hours, salary, number of sick days, raises, benefits, use of the family car, etc., as well as about *general duties* (such as "first and foremost come the children"), but to go beyond that may chase a very good person away.

WELCOMING LETTER, WRITTEN AGREEMENT

Here's an example of an informal written agreement.

March 15, 1989

Ms. Mona Jones
17–76 183rd Street
Cleveland, Ohio   12304

Dear Mona,

Elizabeth, John, and I are thrilled to have you join us. As we agreed, you will begin work Monday, March 23, at 7:15 A.M. A list of your duties follows, along with a breakdown of your compensation.

Responsibilities

- Loving Elizabeth—she's always the first priority.
- Household laundry.
- Housekeeping—dusting, vacuuming, straightening up, bathrooms, making beds (daily), keeping kitchen clean, light cooking.
- Food shopping.
- Occasional errands—dropping off dry cleaning, film, etc.
- Taking Elizabeth to classes.

Compensation

- Gross pay each week (52 weeks) = $240.
- We must deduct $16.08 from the $240 for *your* share of Social Security. We must pay an additional $16.08 for *our* share of your Social Security payments (we file for you).

- Your take-home pay each week will be $223.92. We will also pay for your unemployment insurance and workers' compensation insurance.
- You will be responsible for paying and filing your own taxes.
- You will be paid every Friday. We will pay your food costs Monday–Friday.
- We'd like you to arrive either Sunday evening *or* by 7:15 Monday morning. You're free to leave when we get home Friday evenings. Transportation to and from work is your responsibility.
- You will get 2 weeks (10 working days) of paid vacation, plus holidays such as Christmas, Thanksgiving, Labor Day, and Memorial Day. Your vacation must be taken when we take ours. For example, this year we expect to go away for 8 days in August and we generally take a few days on or around Christmas.
- We also take many 3 and 4 day weekends and we will always give you plenty of notice so you can plan your schedule.
- Time off during the week will be on an informal basis, for example, for an hour when we get home from work, but before dinner.

Please let us know if you have any questions about the above. We welcome you into our home.

Sincerely,
Margaret and John Hall

CARE GIVER INFORMATION YOU SHOULD HAVE IN WRITING

The following is something we definitely suggest every family require in writing from their care giver. Make sure it is completed before your new care giver begins working for you.

An employment form is required virtually everywhere for new employees. But despite its almost universal use in industrial plants, offices, and the civil service, many parents have very little concrete information about the people who take care of their children; some don't even have their childcare person's home phone number. From our own experiences and those of parents we interviewed we strongly advise that you have a written record of personal facts about your new employee, in case of an emergency. This helps ensure the safety and security of everyone involved—you, your child, and your care giver. So whether you're hiring someone to work on-the-books or off, part time or full time, living in your home or out, we urge you to have your care giver fill out a form with some basic information about herself. It should look something like the following.

Name:_____

Address:_____

Phone Number:_____

Social Security Number (if applicable)*_____

Passport or Green Card Number (if applicable)*_____

Driver's License Number and State (if applicable)_____

Name, Address, and Phone Number of Someone to Contact in Case of Emergency: _____

_____

_____

HIRING TEMPORARY HELP

You never know when you're going to need temporary help. We've heard of innumerable instances where a family's regular care giver is unable to work for a period of time; this could be because of maternity leave, illness or injury, immigration problems, or for any number of other reasons. If you're satisfied with your childcare person and want her to return when she's once again able, you will

* If you're hiring on-the-books, you're required to see citizenship or permanent residency documents and social security card.

most likely need someone to take her place for a limited period of time.

A temporary childcare worker is also someone you call in to provide day help when your regular person calls in sick or is otherwise unable to come to work. You have lots of choices when faced with that situation: You can stay home; you can call grandma, an aunt, or a family friend; or you can hire someone from the outside. Even then, networking may pay off; you might find day help through your regular baby sitter or from a friend who has already used the same person. It's a good idea, when possible, to plan for such eventualities in advance; it's always a scramble when you get a call in the morning telling you the baby sitter's not coming, but with some preparation, at least you'll know who to call. And the important thing is that, however you solve the problem of finding a fill-in care giver, you should never compromise your standards of care for your child.

Even if a person's only going to work for you temporarily, it's important that you interview carefully and check references; you're still entrusting them with your children and your home. You may be able to compromise on some skills or attributes (such as language ability with your preschool child), but you can't compromise on trustworthiness. If you're lucky, your own regular person may be able to recommend someone to take her place, but even if the temporary replacement comes with the highest recommendation from your own care giver, it's essential that you speak to her yourself and check her other references before hiring. You don't have to be as thorough in your interviewing as you would be if you were hiring a permanent care giver, but you do have to know that when you leave your home both your child and your possessions are in good hands. So interview and check references when hiring temporary help; it's more than worth the time and effort.

CHAPTER 5

You've Found the Right Person

Monday, 8:20 A.M. You glance at your watch, then you look at your child with more than a little trepidation. Even if you were completely careful in hiring your new care giver, a small, nagging doubt about your decision probably remains. You're a normal parent.

In the days and weeks (and possibly months and years) to come, you'll find out whether your judgment was correct, whether the person who is about to walk through your door will in fact give your child the love and care he needs, and whether she will be a person you can feel comfortable with working in your home. But before the doorbell rings . . .

TWO QUESTIONS MOTHERS ASK MOST

"How will I know my baby knows I'm the mommy?" and "Is my baby going to love the baby sitter more than me?" Fretta Reitzes of New York's 92nd Street Y Parenting Center hears these questions or variants over and over again in her discussions with mothers. She doesn't minimize mothers' concerns, but like many other experts in the field of parenting and child development, she feels that a care giver's relationship to a child should be a loving one and that it's in large part determined by the attitudes and actions of parents.

The relationship between your child's care giver and your family can be very special, combining aspects of employment and familial attachment, self-interest, and love.

Some mothers are afraid of this relationship, fearing that the care giver will replace them in the eyes and in the love of their children. One mother we interviewed, in order to prevent her daughter from becoming too attached to her nanny, replaced her care givers every two or three months. Was that necessary? Was it good for the child?

As long as a mother gives her own love to her children, she can never be replaced. Dr. Irving Sigel of the Educational Testing Service reassures mothers who fear the attachment of their children to care givers, "Mothers do not have mother substitutes. A childcare worker shares the mother's responsibility, but she doesn't take the mother's place. Even when you leave the house you're still the mother."

Dr. Gail Wasserman, who teaches in Columbia University's College of Physicians and Surgeons child psychiatry department, has further words of encouragement for mothers. "Evidence suggests," she says, "that children form attachments not to the people who do the housework and who change their diapers, but to the people who play with them. Two hours of unadulterated free play time is what makes the relationship. This is good news for working mothers."

Your child has the capacity to love more than one person at a time. Psychotherapist Elaine Ruskin says, "Your child knows at a very early age that you're the mother, and it's both to your child's advantage and your own that he has relationships with more than one person." And Susan Kurnit, an instructor at the Parenting Center of the 92nd Street Y, concurs, saying, "From the time a baby is two months old she can react differently to different people." She says

mothers and baby sitters are not and cannot be the same and that
mothers should understand that their babies can be attached in a
different way to their childcare people. "I see babies who call the
baby sitter 'mom,' " says Ms. Kurnit. "But the baby sitters know
that the babies know the difference."

Childbirth educator Charlene Stokamer is emphatic about the
desirability of a loving relationship between child and care giver.
She says that for a child to love the person who acts in the role of the
parent when the parent is gone is ideal not just for the child, but for
the parents as well. She feels that there's no reason to be threatened
by this love, because "there are different kinds of love."

Child psychiatrist Dr. William Koch warns parents against being
competitive with childcare workers, saying, "There's nothing wrong
with attachment to the care giver." As for the question "Is my baby
going to love the baby sitter more than me?" pediatrician Dr. Judy
Goldstein says, "You should only be so lucky. Emotionally, blood is
thicker than water."

Historically, people left their children in the care of a trusted
family member, and many still see that as an ideal childcare situation. Most parents still expect their children to react with love to a
spouse, a grandparent, or another close family member. But the
close-knit extended family of the past has broken down in our time,
and with its disappearance many people have started to look outside the family for childcare. Although there have always been some
people hired to take care of other people's children, there is no
precedent for the sheer numbers of today's parents who have either
chosen or been forced into this position. It's a new, emotionally
complex situation. Parents don't know how to respond, they don't
know how close to get, they don't know how close their children
should get. If your child perceives the care giver in the same positive
way as he would a family member, it's nothing to be afraid of—it's
most likely a sign of a happy child and a healthy relationship.

But is your care giver a member of your family? Most emphatically, no. But reality doesn't prevent you from wanting to view the child-care worker as part of your family, especially if you feel guilty about leaving your child in someone else's care. As Dr. Irving Sigel says, "It makes it easier to leave the child if you know you're leaving him with a family member." It may make it easier, and the feelings are certainly understandable—but it doesn't make it real.

If you project a familial relationship onto a childcare worker you're blurring the real distinctions. Your relationship with your care giver is essentially one of employer and employee. It's a very intimate business relationship, to be sure, but it's business all the same.

Treating an employee as a member of the family (which is not the same as treating her with love and respect) has numerous pitfalls, and the person who in the end suffers the most is likely to be your child. In one family we know of, the care giver was encouraged to feel that she was part of the family. She gradually became more and more possessive of the child (seeing him as her own), and finally declared to the parents that he was the center of her life, that it would kill her to be separated from him. Although this care giver's attachment never reached the point of placing the child in actual jeopardy, it became a serious problem for everyone concerned, and correcting her misapprehension (fostered by the parents) eventually led to bad feelings on all sides.

The need some parents feel to make their childcare workers part of the family often leads to a breakdown of parental authority, with mothers and fathers no longer feeling competent to criticize care givers or really be in control of the kind of care, discipline or education their children receive. For many people this isn't a problem, but if it is for you, there are things you can do to maintain your employer-employee relationship while keeping it special and close.

Some parents declare outright that the primary responsibility of their childcare employee is to love their child; this allows, even encourages, a closeness to exist, but places it outside the realm of the family.

Many other parents distance themselves from their care givers by the use of names; how you address someone affects how you perceive and treat them. Some parents give themselves titles of authority (Mrs., Mr., Dr.), others address their care givers in a similar manner, and some people do both.

In addition, if your child is old enough to comprehend, the role of the care giver should be made as clear as possible: She is someone hired to take care of you (the child); we hope she will pay attention to you, care for you, and love you. She is a very special person in your life, but she has a life of her own that's separate from yours and from the life of our family.

The explanation may be a little difficult to get across, particularly if your care giver lives in, but it's still important that your child understand. How do you accomplish this? Perhaps you could explain to your child about the care giver's time off, or you could get him or her involved in certain aspects of the employment process itself. In addition, your care giver herself may be enlisted in helping define the boundaries of the relationship. For example, if you encourage her to show photographs and tell your child about where she came from (whether it be Ireland, the Caribbean, or Mexico), it will help get across that her background and identity is different from yours and your child's.

Here are two families' solutions: One little girl talks to her care giver's husband on the phone and a little boy knows his childcare person's daughter and at the end of the day says goodbye to his care giver with the full knowledge that she's going home to be with her own family. These two children are not yet three years old, yet they have no problems handling this knowledge about their care givers. It doesn't make them feel any less love or attachment to the people who care for them when their parents are away.

Many children, when they reach the age of two and a half or three, pick up the family baby sitter distinction almost by osmosis. As they move into a social world of childcare workers and children, they see that there's a difference between their parents' friends and their care giver's friends. And if their care givers give them love, it's not hard for them to love their care givers in return—as a primary person in their lives who is not a member of the family.

SETTING THE TONE

Monday, 8:30 A.M. The doorbell rings, and you let your new care giver into your home, and into your lives. The next step is to start to get to know each other, finding out what makes her tick and letting her in on what you and your children need from her. Everybody has to get used to each other, and you, the parents, are a key ingredient in that process.

Children react differently to different people; their relationships are not interchangeable. Don't expect your child to act in exactly the same way to a new childcare person as he or she did to her former baby sitter, or as he or she does to you. Your child may act out fears of being abandoned, may be angry and feel shunted around from person to person, or may be overjoyed at having a wonderful new person around. Children's responses are not predictable, but you can make the transition easier for them by being aware of their feelings.

There may well be times, particularly in the next few weeks, when you'll be needed to act as intermediaries, to explain your children's responses and needs to this new person in their lives. In making the transition, it's important that your children not feel that someone is being forced on them. Allow them and their new care giver the time to warm up to each other at their own paces.

If you want your child to respect and respond to a childcare person in a positive way, all the experts we've spoken with agree that you yourself must set an example and treat the childcare person with respect. Your sensitivity to everyone's feelings—your child's, your care giver's, and your own—will be an important first step in making this new relationship work—for everyone.

TRAINING AND ORIENTATION

You may have given your new care giver a letter outlining her duties when you hired her or you may have been more comfortable with an "informal" verbal contract. Whichever the case, it's no longer enough. There's a lot more to do, both in terms of attitudes and in translating generalizations into the nitty-gritty details of everyday life.

It is hoped that you can take some time to be with your child and his new care giver. If you race out of the house the minute she arrives it's hard to have any input, to be able to help with the transition, or even to know what's happening. We're aware that making this time available is often difficult in households with two working parents (or in households where there is a single parent), but it's very important that you, or some other responsible adult who is intimate with you and your children, be at home now. (If you're replacing a care giver who is leaving on good terms, try having the new person start before the old one is gone; that way the departing childcare worker can aid in the training and transition period.)

Your job at this time includes making your specific wishes clear from the very beginning, as well as reiterating the needs you stated when you interviewed and hired your new care giver. Amplify, explain, clarify. Take nothing for granted.

Introduce her to the neighborhood: Show her where the playground is, where to shop for groceries, and the best route to the children's school. If it matters to you, show her exactly how you want things done (even down to details such as how you want the laundry folded). Explain your household schedule: Tell her when the children eat, when you want them to nap, and what you want done when.

There is no reason to assume that your new care giver will intuitively know what you want, but there's plenty of reason to assume that she won't. Every family is different, both in the ways that they interact and in everyday details. For example, what does your child like to eat for lunch (or what do you want him to eat)? If you leave the choices about food up to your care giver, it would be unreasonable to be angry about her choices. If your child requires a special diet, tell your care giver. If you have other special dietary needs (such as maintaining a household that's kosher or vegetarian), explain them to her because she has no other way of knowing.

Some people need a lot of direction; others take responsibility from the moment they arrive. Just because a person is one way or another doesn't mean she won't be perfectly wonderful once she understands the needs of your household. If she needs help, help her to understand. And when you see something you don't like, say so right away. If you let it sit, it becomes set.

You have to decide how much authority your care giver will have in running your household, from calling the plumber to setting up your child's social calendar to deciding what your child eats or even how your child is disciplined. If you don't make decisions, you're abdicating your responsibility (which is a decision in itself).

Over and over in our research, both childcare workers and parents have suggested sitting down together right away when a new person begins work to discuss children's *current needs* and how they affect the job. Virtually everyone agrees that some things should be left open-ended, or at least subject to change, because as children grow, their needs (and thus the optimal arrangement between you and your care giver) change. For example, a healthy newborn sleeps most of the day; a person taking care of a newborn baby may thus have plenty of time to clean and cook. But an active toddler needs much more supervision; to give him the extra attention he requires will in all likelihood cause other tasks to fall by the wayside. And when a child is of school age, his care giver, freed from all-day supervision, will once again have more time to take care of the house.

Don't expect more from your childcare person than you would from yourself. As one observant Boston mother told us, "Many of our baby sitter's friends tell us that they do not feel comfortable with their employers, that they feel people try to get the most work for the least money and that employers are most concerned with the 'visible' aspects of the job, for example they focus on the fact that there is dust on the coffee table rather than appreciating that the baby sitter comforted a teething child all afternoon. There are too many impossible 'Mary Poppins' demands placed on people who work caring for children."

If it's at all possible, we recommend a training period of about two weeks (during which a parent or other knowledgeable adult is home). Many people, particularly in families led by a single parent or in two-working-parent households, can't take this much time. If that's the case with you, don't feel guilty about it (you still have to make a living)—but try to be there as much as you can.

During this period of acclimation for your children and their new care giver, it's very helpful to arrange some time where there's some real three-way interaction. It helps your children feel comfortable and secure, it helps your care giver learn how you take care of your children (by seeing how you comfort, how you play, how you discipline), and it helps you to teach your new childcare worker how you want things done and to learn how she will act in everyday situations with your children. In addition (even if you're unable to be around for any extended period), you should try to be in and out as much as possible in order to observe and guide the development of the interaction between your children and their childcare person.

THE TRIAL PERIOD

The training period is a time to make your wishes clear, to let your new care giver know what is required of her on a day-to-day basis and to start to get to know each other. After the training period is over you probably won't be home as much; you may be returning to work or be reinvolving yourself in other activities. In any case, you'll probably be leaving the care of your children in her hands for extended periods of time.

This is the crucial stage in a family's relationship to a care giver when perceptive parents see how well the new person is working out, whether she's doing what's been asked of her, and how the children are responding to her presence. It's a time to make adjustments, if necessary, and to try to help the person do her job better. It's also a time to evaluate a childcare worker's performance and to decide whether a permanent arrangement with her is really going to work.

Except for a trial period imposed by an agency (which often collects its fee after a specified period of employment), the time you spend evaluating a new care giver is basically unannounced. But agency-imposed or self-imposed, a trial period most definitely exists. Many parents feel that after just a few weeks they know whether or not a relationship with a childcare worker will work out. In any case, after observing and adjusting, explaining and interacting for two or three months, you should be relatively certain whether an arrangement will work on a long-term basis.

During the first few weeks of employment, a care giver is often on her best behavior, but even if she is trying to impress you now (and is likely to relax more later), the tone you set during this time should continue even after the trial period is over. Remember, you are still getting to know each other, and you're probably finding out more about each other's personalities every day.

WHEN YOU'RE NOT AROUND

It's essential that you feel secure about what's happening at home when you're not around. Most parents feel they need to have complete trust in their care givers, but it's easier to feel that trust when you really know someone—when her responses are predictable and acceptable, when her explanations are clear and comprehensible, when her ability to take initiative responsibly (or to carry out your directions) are undoubted.

During the trial period, there are several ways to find out what's happening when you're not home. If your children are old enough, you can ask them—but children often have a hidden agenda of their own. You can—and should—call home frequently to speak with your care giver and your children. On the phone you can give instructions, explain your plans, and listen. (If you're concerned that your care giver is spending her day watching the soaps, or that she's plopping your kids down to soak up cartoons when you think they should be playing, you might listen for the drone of the television when you call.)

Sometime during the day you may come home unexpectedly and let yourself in. Some parents feel that this is "spying," and that it's unethical to "spy" on a childcare worker. But there are ways of doing it without feeling that you're doing something wrong, for example, by simply telling her in advance that you may be coming home unexpectedly on occasion.

You or your friends may observe your childcare person and your child in the playground or your friends may drop by, bringing something you left at their houses. If you are seriously distrustful or frightened about leaving your child with someone—anyone—you may even leave your tape recorder on "record" for a couple of hours during the day.

Parents, care givers, and professionals caution against taking any single observation too seriously. Of course, if the child has been placed in real jeopardy by the care giver, either through an oversight or an action, it's not to be taken at all lightly. But short of placing the child in danger, think about it: There may be times when you yourself don't pay complete attention to your children, times when you don't feel well and are irritable, and times when you're distracted. Is it reasonable to judge someone else by standards that are so high you couldn't realistically meet them yourself?

Another mitigating consideration in judging other people's criticisms of your childcare worker is that any person you talk to is likely to bring his or her own biases into what should be a dispassionate observation. In fact, Fretta Reitzes warns that parents' friends may be a childcare worker's harshest critics. She counsels that parents should take others' statements with a grain of salt and thinks it's also wise to listen for comments from a cleaning man, a delivery person, a doorman—people who see your childcare person and child together regularly, but who have no particular biases.

The experiences of one mother of our acquaintance brought this point home quite clearly. She had enrolled her two-year-old daughter in an art class, most of the time taking her to class herself but occasionally leaving that task to her child's care giver. One day another mother in the class called to say that she was concerned about the nanny's lack of responsiveness and her surly behavior. The mother thanked her for calling but, after thinking about it, didn't take the advice too much to heart—she knew her nanny was essentially shy in group situations and remembered that the nanny had a severe cold the last time she took the girl to class. In addition, almost everyone else who spoke about her daughter's relationship with her nanny noticed their mutual affection and the ease with which they related to each other.

This is not to say that your observations (or those of your friends) are groundless. It's just that you should put each separate observation into the context of what you already know, so that you neither jump to conclusions nor ignore real evidence.

A suburban mother we interviewed told us that after coming home from work one afternoon, she asked her new nanny where she had gone during the course of the day. The nanny replied, "Nowhere," but the odometer on the car said otherwise—she had put on over a hundred miles that day, and worse yet, had lied about it. The nanny was asked to explain what really happened, her explanation was accepted, and she was given another chance.

In another case, the childcare worker was not given a second chance. This time the mother came home in the middle of the afternoon and went directly to the neighborhood playground, where she hoped to observe her three-year-old and his care giver at a distance. She did see the baby sitter, speaking with a group of other childcare workers, but she couldn't locate her son. She couldn't find him because he had run out of the playground—he was on the street alone and the person entrusted with his care hadn't even noticed. She was fired on the spot.

Another mother was informed by a neighbor that her au pair was taking an aerobics class each morning, leaving her children with another neighborhood care giver. After checking the facts, the parents gave the au pair the message that any extracurricular activities during work hours were entirely at their discretion—if the au pair wanted to do something for herself during that time she had to clear it first, and if she didn't she would be fired.

Sometimes problems during the trial period are due to lack of communication. For example, if you come home and your house is spotless, you may have wrongly given the message to the care giver that the housework—not the children—comes first. If this is the case, the best way to proceed is to just reiterate your priorities.

PLANNING FOR CONTINGENCIES

There are so many unknown factors when you hire a new childcare person that it's wise to leave space for adjustment. Unless you've had years of experience with in-home help, you probably won't have any guidelines to use for questions such as telephone usage, food allowances, use of the family car, or socialization during work time.

In addition (and this particularly holds true for live-in arrangements), you have no idea how her way of life will affect you. If you add new rules after the training period, *she* may feel taken advantage of, but if you don't, *you* may feel taken advantage of.

We know of one family where a live-in person who was new to the United States was hired. As she had no roots or personal relationships in the city where she was now working or living, the parents felt it was unnecessary to discuss her personal life with her when they hired her. But as she got to know people, she began to have friends, and eventually she started seeing a man. He began to visit her often in the evenings and at times during the day (when she was watching the children) as well. The parents, concerned both that her relationship with her boyfriend was cutting into the attention she paid to the children and that her boyfriend's frequent presence was an intrusion into their lives, set down new rules about his visits. The childcare worker responded with anger, feeling that the rules were completely arbitrary. She argued that when she was hired there were no constraints on her social life and wondered why the parents had suddenly changed their minds. On their part, the parents felt completely justified; they hadn't made rules previously because the reality of the situation didn't include any need for them.

Of course it's best to make as much as possible clear from the very beginning, but it's not always possible. You can't know that she'll become depressed when her parents come to town, fall in love, or get pregnant. If you hired live-in help, and you've never had anyone live in before, you may not know yourself how you will respond to another person's presence in your home. One mother, who has had both live-in and live-out childcare help, explained the difference. "Live-in people are in your space," she said. "Boundaries are more difficult to set up. You have to worry about their needs . . . is there food in the house? Are they warm and comfortable? You also wake up in the morning and see someone else right away."

There are literally hundreds of unforseen problems that can crop up and that thoroughly defy prediction, but with a little bit of forethought you can avoid a situation such as this one a Philadelphia mother told us about. "Having a person in my house who left filled ashtrays and dirty dishes in the sink was more than I wanted to deal with," she said. "Although she was really good at childcare I couldn't stand the situation and let her go."

Many parents try to build in a level of flexibility, both in terms of hours and duties, from the very beginning. And childcare workers who are asked to be flexible tend to be more contented and willing if some of the flexibility is reciprocal. One angry baby sitter said, "I'm hardly ever late; but every once in a while because of traffic I'm late and she's incensed. . . . Meanwhile, three nights a week she calls and tells me she's going to be late because she's stuck in a meeting."

AT THE END OF THE TRIAL PERIOD

If you have not had insurmountable problems with your new care giver during the trial period, at its end you should be ready to settle down into a level of security, certainty, and permanence. If you don't expect the world (just a caring, competent person) and you're committed to making the relationship work, it is hoped that you will now be able to look forward to a long-term commitment between you and your care giver. If you're lucky it will work out like it did for a New Jersey mother of three, who said, "After ironing out some initial problems, we have a wonderful relationship—as good as any."

At the end of the trial period, you'll be evaluating whether you want your baby sitter to continue working for you. Over and over we've heard people say that the best way to make this evaluation is to "go with your gut feeling about whether it's working." Because so much of your decision is subjective and based on emotional responses, deciding on the basis of emotions seems to make more sense to most people than making a purely intellectual determination.

Many parents feel that the need for evaluation is mutual. "When hiring," one Los Angeles mother said, "we have a one-month probationary period on both sides and after a month we evaluate the situation and each other." The reasoning is that if your care giver is unhappy, it's not going to work out any better than if you are unhappy.

At the end of the trial period people tend to let their hair down with each other a little more. They settle in and become more relaxed and comfortable. This is partly a function of getting to know each other better and partly the result of your decision to make the arrangement permanent.

At this time many people also increase benefits or give their care givers a raise (as at the end of probationary periods in office jobs). And if the relationship is going to continue to grow and your child is going to get the best available care, this is also a time to ensure that lines of communication remain open.

CHAPTER 6

Making the Relationship Work

As people get to know each other better, they gradually become familiar with each other's ways. After a month or two, you'll probably be more comfortable with your care giver's personality and personal habits, more trusting of her judgment, more aware of her probable responses to a variety of situations involving your children and your home. In all likelihood, she'll also be more aware of the particular needs, desires, and personality traits of both you and your children. Your kids will also have made an adjustment, interacting with (and possibly even growing attached to) the new individual entrusted with their care.

The period of settling in after the trial period is a completely natural part of the process that adds up to a relationship. It's a phase when everyone's already gotten to know each other to some extent, a time when the long-term nature of the relationships—between child and care giver, between parents and care giver—starts taking form.

116

But settling in isn't like falling into a comfortable old chair. It still takes work to keep things moving on the right track; you need to make a thousand little adjustments so that your children can get everything from the care giver that she has to give. Settling in doesn't mean you stop talking, that you stop telling the baby sitter what you need. It doesn't mean that you stop listening either. And by no means does settling in mean that you start settling for less.

THE ART OF COMPROMISE

The person you hired to take care of your children is still only human, even if she is now your employee. She's not a clone or a robot; like all people, she has her strengths and weaknesses. It is hoped that you had some awareness of her strong and weak points when you hired her; now you probably know much more about what makes her tick, what you can count on her to do, and what tasks she is unable, or unwilling, to handle.

Many parents we spoke with echoed the Chicago mother who told us that one of the essential aspects of working with in-home childcare was to "ascertain in advance your areas of flexibility and your absolute requirements." In other words, what trade-offs you're willing to make in order to get the kind of care your child needs.

"I wish she would clean more and follow my arrangement for the closets," bemoaned one New York mother. "But it seems trivial," she continued, "in comparison to how great she is with Stephanie."

Other parents talk about how they wish their housekeepers would iron, how they would like their baby sitters to take more initiative, how they would prefer that their care givers read more to the children. But these parents have accepted that the people who work for them have limitations. If every task is equal in importance—an absolute requirement—then nobody will satisfy you. In order for the care giver/parent relationship to work, you have to recognize, and work with, her limitations. You have to determine which of hundreds of specific things are necessities and which are simply preferences.

A British nanny gave us her own list of pluses when it comes to employers. "Number one, flexibility; number two, letting me adore their kids; number three, a sense of humor; number four, tolerance when I char the kids' dinner."

Sometimes some of the small dissatisfactions that are virtually inevitable in any childcare situation can be overcome. In specific situations where there is conflict between parent and care giver there can also be compromise.

One family was about to leave on a combination vacation/business trip. Their baby sitter had agreed to accompany them, but under pressure from her husband, she reneged within days of their scheduled departure. The parents were furious, with no time to make alternate childcare arrangements. At first they were ready to fire the baby sitter on the spot; then they began to evaluate their real needs and to renegotiate with their sitter (to whom their daughter was very attached). They offered the sitter time off with no pay; she finally reluctantly agreed to go with them (in return for extra pay and subsequent time off).

In many situations, small failings pale in significance when parents look at the whole picture. One suburban Chicago mother told us that her child's nanny "does so much more than the basics: She teaches him numbers, reads to him, takes him on long walks, plays games. Her job is to give him a safe, happy, warm environment during the day—a big job—and she's superior at it." Her one complaint is that the nanny doesn't know how to drive. Another mother and father, faced with a similar situation (of a superior care giver without a driver's license), took it on themselves to teach her how to drive. This answered the parents' need for someone who could do errands and drop off and pick up the child at school, *and* it gave the baby sitter new responsibilities and a greater sense of self-esteem.

COMMUNICATING MAKES IT WORK

The basis of any successful in-home childcare situation is trust; if you're not able to trust your care giver, you can't possibly feel comfortable leaving your children alone with her. The basis of trust is communication. Speak up and let her know what you want and need, clear the air when something bothers you—no one can read anyone else's mind, so if you want her to respond you have to tell her about whatever it is that's in your head.

One Connecticut mother told us why she felt her family's relationship with their care giver worked. "We communicate very easily with one another about everything," she said, "so nothing ever festers. My husband and I actively promote that aspect of our relationship with her since many of the problems our friends have seem to stem from misunderstandings and a lack of clarity about the responsibilities of the baby sitter's job."

Communication: It's essential, even if it's not always easy. Susan Kurnit, who teaches a park-bench course for care givers and children at New York's 92nd Street Y, says, "We need to be educated on how to ask for things. Parents don't want to alienate their childcare people and they don't want to make them angry. So they bend over backward to be nice and sweet."

Both Ms. Kurnit and Dr. William Koch agree that much of the problem with communication is that many middle-class parents are ambivalent about their own role as parents, as well as about how they should act in relation to the mostly working-class care givers they hire. It's not like we're living in the world of "Upstairs, Downstairs," where everyone—masters and servants—have clearly defined roles in an established social hierarchy. Our world is much more complicated than that.

So what, in fact, are your respective roles? You're not master and servant and, for that matter, you are not likely to be exact social and economic equals. (One Chicago mother who hired someone of her own background said that the childcare person "regarded me as her peer and friend and it was hard to give her instructions. She thought she knew everything about child development." The lack of clearly defined roles, as well as the inability of the mother to say, "This is my child, and this is how I want things done," resulted in an unhappy experience for everyone.)

You are employer and employee, united in the principal task of caring for children—your children—who never stop being your responsibility, even when you're off at work and they're in another person's hands. Whenever you talk with your care giver, whenever you compromise, make demands, or come to conclusions about how things are going, always remember what she is there for: to take care of your child. Putting anything else (from your friendship with your care giver to your superior social position) above what's best for your child is a disservice to a person who is totally reliant on you.

It's in this spirit that Fretta Reitzes of New York's 92nd Street Y's Parenting Center says, "You owe it to your care giver and to your child to find ways to talk about your child." If you have problems finding the time to talk with your childcare person about what goes on during the day, try to set aside some time—even a half hour— one day a week. Or speak with her on the telephone, either when your child naps or in the evening when you're back in your respective homes. These conversations—in which your child's care giver shares her everyday experiences and observations of your child with you and you share your wishes, ideas, and views about how you want things done with her—are important, and there's no one they're more important to than your child.

Dr. Koch told us of a conversation he recently overheard between two couples on a commuter train. One mother was complaining to her traveling companion about her childcare woes: It was beginning to appear to her that her child's caretaker literally parks herself and her son in front of the television most of the day; the baby sitter also seems to be feeding him a menu consisting exclusively of pasta with ketchup. The other woman suggested that the mother make up a schedule of things for her baby sitter to do with her child and also suggested that she prepare a menu for the care giver to follow. The father, unwilling to be involved himself in such mundane matters, said, "Yes dear, why don't you do that?" And the mother responded by saying she didn't have the time.

The story of this commuter couple is in stark contrast with the involvement of the Los Angeles working mother who told us, "We discuss my child's behavior and growth regularly and I encourage her to tell me how the day was and what happened. From the information she gives me, I let her know what I like. And if there is something that went on that I don't like, I tell her *why*."

How is this mother able to maintain such an open, honest relationship with her care giver? Her answer is quite simple.

MUTUAL RESPECT

This mother believes her childcare arrangement works because it's based on "mutual respect." Many professionals in the field of child development express similar opinions, stating that it's important not only for you and your care giver, but that it is essential for the development of self-esteem in your child. Dr. Koch, for example, told us how some parents treat childcare people with disrespect and yet expect their children to treat their baby sitters with respect. "If you eat steak and give them bologna," explains Dr. Koch, your child will get the message. The problem is it's a confusing message, one that leaves a child wondering where he is in the pecking order. A child, who needs love, time, concern, and the certainty that his parents care for him, may end up believing that because you are leaving him with an inferior person, that he too must be inferior.

A relationship need not be egalitarian to be respectful. But it does mean listening to what the care giver has to say. One care giver asked a mom to obtain an easier stroller for her to use on the subway and bus. The request was refused, and the care giver saw it as a direct slap—as though the parents were saying, "We don't care what you think you need." This and other similar instances made her feel unwanted and unappreciated and drove her to look for another job.

Respect also means not expecting her to do something you yourself could not, or would not, do. One nanny, based in San Francisco, told us this story. "I was working for a family who had a cabin in the mountains. One night they and their friends went out together, and left me to take care of all their kids. I was alone in this cabin with ten kids, ranging in age from eight months to thirteen years. You can imagine what I felt. Anyway, I didn't express my unhappiness because I felt intimidated . . . but I left as soon as I could."

Respecting your childcare person doesn't mean that you should consider her to be interchangeable with yourselves. People are simply not interchangeable in that way; each of us has her own strengths and weaknesses, her own particular ways of doing things, her own endearing and annoying qualities. If your care giver's ways are different from yours, but not in conflict with yours, then there's nothing wrong with them.

One care giver asked us to give this advice to parents: "Parents should remember that children have a different repertoire with childcare people." Your child will respond to his father and his mother differently; he'll have a different attitude with his grandmother than with his teacher. He may have activities that he prefers doing with you and others that are more fun with the baby sitter. For example, he may sing only with mom, play computer games only with dad, and paint only with nanny. Or he may have a favorite book he likes mom to read and another he likes nanny to read.

One Washington mother said about her childcare person, "She's very, very special but she's not family. My relationship with her is sometimes employer-employee, sometimes friend. I don't expect her to be a substitute for me, and I don't expect her to necessarily be able to handle things as I would, as long as there's no *gross* difference (hitting, lack of affection, etc.). But she respects me and I respect her—I feel that's why we've been together for seven years."

In another case, a successful professional couple with a sixty-year-old care giver from the Dominican Republic wrote to us about why their arrangement has worked for almost a decade. "The personality of our baby sitter is special: She doesn't do everything exactly the way we do, but she's very responsible, which allows us the freedom to not watch how everything is handled. We trust her. Whatever arrangement you agree on, the success of the relationship has most to do with the quality of the *person*—their honesty, warmth, and work ethic—not their country of origin, training, or language." And, as is evident from this couple's words, it also has a lot to do with the ability of the employer to appreciate, and express appreciation, for the important job being done by the childcare employee.

Pediatrician Dr. Judy Goldstein says, "What makes the relationship work with a childcare person is caring for her as a person, and rewarding her for good work. It enhances her self-esteem to know she's being appreciated." She suggests that one of the principal ways appreciation and concern can be expressed is in gifts. Professionals and parents alike agree that everyone appreciates a "thank you" and an acknowledgment of how well they're doing on the job.

SEEING THINGS FROM YOUR CARE GIVER'S POINT OF VIEW

Part of making it work is having a simple understanding of, and sympathy for, your care giver's situation. In the questionnaire we distributed to childcare workers, we asked the question, "What advice would you give parents about working with a childcare person?" Over and over we got similar responses: "Put yourself in her shoes," "Try to imagine doing what you ask your baby sitter to do," "Don't underestimate how important and responsible the job is." So for a moment, put yourself in her shoes.

Heather, an English nanny, told us, "It's hard to keep yourself motivated. I sometimes say, 'God, I've had an awful day,' but then I think about all the funny things that happened. And then I don't feel like it's a job at all."

Put yourself in her shoes, not only in terms of the work, or her relationship with your child, or the money, but in terms of her emotional life as well. Recognizing her as a person with needs of her own and having genuine regard and sensitivity for her feelings, making adjustments when possible in order to accommodate her, and arranging interesting activities for her and your children—even the simple act of treating her fairly—these are all ways that you can strengthen the bonds between yourself and your childcare worker without seriously compromising your needs and the needs of your children. And you don't have to be a psychologist to know that someone to whom you give consideration will be more likely to return the favor and go the extra mile for you when you need it.

A New Jersey family with an au pair said, "We provide a lot of flexibility with regard to her 'special needs.' For example, she takes college courses two evenings a week and we work around it; she wanted to give a party and we said 'no problem;' she calls home (to Montana) weekly at our expense." None of these accommodations have been extremely difficult for this particular family, on the contrary the benefits far outweigh the hardships. Their willingness to give has given them a contented care giver who will work evenings when asked, who will take on extra responsibilities without resentment, and who will give more of herself on a day-to-day basis in her job.

Soon after their baby was born, a New York family with two

preteenagers (it was a second family for one of the spouses) started looking for a care giver. After a relatively long search, they hired a woman whom they considered to be the best, most competent, and most trustworthy person they had seen. The woman, who lived in a ghetto area, had two younger school-age children of her own. After school, she arranged for her kids to be taken care of by a neighborhood woman, but she worried constantly about their well-being and the quality of their education. After a while, the employers, by saying that their sitter lived with them, arranged for her kids to attend a much better school in their neighborhood and to come over to their house after school. "Although it's stressful having them here every day," the baby's mother told us, "it's less stressful than having her anxious about their baby sitter picking them up after school every day." This arrangement, now well into its second year, seems to be working for everyone. The care giver is secure about her children, thus allowing her greater flexibility; when the little girl's parents are forced to work late, the sitter gladly stays, unperturbed by questions about her own children's care or safety. And there's an added bonus: The care giver's children dote on the preschooler.

In Seattle, a family hired a care giver who had a daughter of her own one month older than their infant son. The woman took care of both children in the employer's home. "This was very helpful to his socialization," the parents told us, as it "kept him from getting too spoiled."

A Boston care giver's parents came up from Jamaica to stay with her for several months. It was an eventful stay: The care giver's parents fought incessantly; one of them had an extended illness that required hospitalization; and the care giver and her own school-age daughter were forced to share a room. In the end, the longest time this woman had spent with her parents since childhood was an extremely difficult time for her. Although she was depressed, and her functioning at work diminished as a result, the family for whom she worked recognized that the stress was temporary, and they rode

out the storm with her. She was, after all, a very special and important person to their children.

A New York family gave their care giver maternity leave, hiring a
temporary replacement. It was a stressful few months for their
children (saying goodbye, having to get used to someone new, and
then having to reorient themselves to their permanent person's
return), but the parents felt that because their regular sitter was
such a loving and trustworthy person, it was worth making adjustments to keep her with their family.

It's important to remember that your care giver has a family life,
and an emotional life, that's separate from your own. For example,
an au pair or nanny can get homesick. An English girl, away from
her own family for the first time, may feel culture shock and need to
make that occasional phone call home to "her mum." A woman from
Jamaica, forced by economic circumstances to temporarily leave her
own children in the care of another family member back home, may
miss them, worry about their welfare, even get depressed because
of her separation from them.

To treat someone fairly means to respect her as a human being
with needs of her own. For example, if you go away for the summer
it's unreasonable and unfair to leave your permanent childcare
worker without work and money; she still has to eat. And if you
don't pay her during your extended vacation, you'd be foolish to
assume that she'll still be there when you need her at the end of
summer. Treating someone fairly can also be its own reward.

Keep Lines of Communication Open

Elaine Ruskin thinks that "mutual respect" means just what the
words say—that it should go both ways. "From the childcare person's point of view," says Ms. Ruskin, "she should be trying to
enhance the mom's relationship with the baby."

Care givers who are working at making it work will keep lines of communication open as well. They will recognize the parents' primacy in the household, yet they will also be aware that they too have something to contribute besides just their physical presence. They will tell parents about their children's developmental changes, suggest different ways problems can be handled, take on new responsibilities without having everything spelled out. These types of independent action on the part of care givers are a sign of self-respect, and as long as they are done in consultation with children's guardians, they also show respect and care for the employing family.

YOUR BABY SITTER'S FRIENDS

Your care giver has friends of her own, both during work time and away from your family. When she is at work, she is most likely to have associations, acquaintances, and friendships with other people doing similar work. This has an effect both on her perception of her job and on your child's social life.

In terms of her perception of the job: If she is being paid less than her friends for the same work, she is sure to become dissatisfied with her arrangement with you and if she is the only one required to do housework, she's likely to ask for a renegotiation of the contract. You can bet that if you don't know the norms in your community for childcare workers' salaries and duties, your baby sitter will let you know after she's met some of her neighborhood peers. But it works both ways: You may be the example your care giver's friends bring up in their negotiations; she may also realize that you are more generous, more thoughtful, and more reasonable than most of her fellow care givers' employers.

As for the effect your childcare worker's friendships have on your child's social life: To a very large extent (particularly with very young children), the people your baby sitter befriends will determine the kids your child plays with. Probably as many early childhood friendships result from care givers' relationships with other care givers as from parents' relationships with other parents.

This can be an advantage. It may open up your child's social world to include people you might not know yourselves. If your baby sitter is a good, caring person, she will most likely associate with other similar people. You might even meet, and become friendly with, the parents yourselves.

And, if the people you are already friendly with have as good judgment in hiring people as you do, her friends and yours may parallel each other. As one Seattle mother said, "Arranging play dates has been easy. Her sister takes care of a child in the neighborhood the same age as ours and she's become friendly with the baby sitter of our son's best friend."

SPENDING TIME TOGETHER

If you want your children to get the message that there is mutual respect between you and their baby sitter it's a good idea to arrange for a time during the week when you're all together. Playing together has other rewards as well: You can observe how your children and their care giver interact, it keeps lines of communication open, and it enables you to be in a position to make suggestions, based on firsthand experience, of things you would like changed.

One thing to be aware of is that your child may play you off your care giver; although it can be unsettling, it's a perfectly normal response from a child and not an indication that something is wrong. This "playing one off the other" behavior may be even more pronounced if the mother is home—one British nanny we interviewed wouldn't take a job for a family with a nonworking mother because she felt this form of conflict was exacerbated by the constant presence of the mother. Because most children view their mothers as their principal care giver, the nanny felt that her authority and ability to function autonomously with the children in her care was sure to be undermined simply by the mother's presence.

DAILY TRANSITIONS

"Everytime you leave your child it's like a mini mourning," family therapist Dr. Sandra Rodman Mann told us. Yet many parents arrange childcare schedules so that the moment the care giver arrives in the morning, the parents leave (and the moment they return in the afternoon she's out the door).

If it's at all possible, schedule your childcare worker's arrival and departure to allow your children a few minutes of overlap, so that they can have the chance to make a smooth and easy transition of their own, both morning and evening.

At the very least, prepare yourself and your schedule to allow for these periods of separation and transition. For example, if your baby sitter comes to work at 8:30 and you have to leave for the office immediately on her arrival, yet you know your child feels more secure when you read him a book before you go in the morning, then be ready to sit down to read to him at 8:20. When the baby sitter arrives, have her read a second book to your child. Make sure you're ready to go early enough so that you can have that undistracted time with your child. Plan for it; get your clothes or your child's clothes laid out the night before. If need be, shower at night rather than in the morning. Then you won't feel like you're running out and your child won't feel like you're abandoning him.

When working parents come home at the end of the day, they often find it very difficult to leave the office behind and become immediately and completely responsive to their children.

Some parents take a few minutes to cool out after work. They feel that it's time well spent, a transition time that enables them to really be available and responsive once they're with their children. One New York City working mother told us she changes her clothes, washes her face, and puts on her sneakers before she leaves the office; a father takes a leisurely three-mile walk home each day, thus allowing himself to arrive home with the stresses of the day behind him.

Kids may be different from grown-ups, but they're not all *that* different; it's as difficult for them to switch gears on a moment's notice as it is for you. Elaine Ruskin says, "At the end of the day some kids become aggressive or withdrawn. It's typical—perfectly natural and expected—for them to have difficulty reconnecting." She recommends that parents allow their children "to just be. Don't force them to behave or react the way you want." She cautions that if they're not given the space they need they may then have feelings of being cut off and misunderstood.

Dr. William Koch agrees, advising that parents allow their children to come to them at the end of the day. Depending on your child, he says, "you may have to let him warm up to you. You may have a happy bubbling child, yet he may be angry for the first twenty minutes when you get home—every day." He also suggests that you make sure you are free from other responsibilities and ready to spend quality time with your child when you get home.

As to how to make the transition work, Dr. Irving Sigel says, "Don't put your children on the spot" when you get home. Don't say, "were you a good boy today?," or "did you get along with nanny," or "how was school today?" Instead say, "Hi, how are you doing? What's up?" Ask them what kind of day they had today. Tell them about the interesting things that happened to you today. In short, engage them, don't confront them. *"It's the sharing that's important,"* concludes Dr. Sigel.

In addition, one English nanny we interviewed insists on "debriefing" the parents at the end of the day—whether it takes five minutes or a half hour. This may work for your family, but if your child really needs your attention it may be a transitional solution for you and your care giver but not for your child. If your child wants *you* when you come home, she may not want to share you with her baby sitter.

A Detroit man solved this problem by speaking on the telephone with his childcare person two evenings a week and by leaving a notebook in a prominent place at home for her to jot down her impressions as well as concrete day-by-day events. The notebook had headings for meal times and food served, nap times, diaper changes, play activities and playdates, and the child's reactions and emotional state. Evening telephone conversations were reserved for discussions about child development, child-rearing philosophy, and discipline.

DISCIPLINE

Ideas about proper discipline vary from culture to culture, from class to class, even from individual to individual within a particular social group. The range of attitudes in one New York play group of six upper-middle-class mothers and their preschool children is not unusual: Their views on discipline range all the way from the practice of light corporal punishment to never saying no to the child (and encompass virtually everything in between). So it's no wonder that questions of discipline, punishment, and the setting of limits are often very sticky problems for parents and care givers.

One Oregon father told us, "The most difficult problem is to get the sitter to share your philosophy regarding discipline and to participate in its execution. Too often they completely refrain from discipline and children get out of control." But this father is the exception that proves the rule; we've come across many more cases where the philosophical roles are reversed.

Indeed, one of the most frequent complaints we've encountered from childcare workers about their employers is that the parents spoil their children, that they allow them to get away with too much and that they don't discipline them enough. Some psychiatric and social work professionals agree with this analysis; they say many working mothers have a tendency to be lenient because they feel guilty about not being at home themselves.

Whatever the reasons for your attitudes, they're yours, and the responsibility for how your child is disciplined is yours alone. It's important for you to feel comfortable about your attitudes toward limits and discipline, and it's essential to your child that there be consistency in the way your attitudes are implemented. Keeping the need for consistency in mind, it's very possible that you will hire a baby sitter whose perspective is different from yours. What's important, however, is not what she believes, it's what she does—she must follow your lead in the way she disciplines your children; you must ensure that her actions are completely consistent with your own.

One nanny told us, "I believe in smacking a kid when he does something wrong; then it's over and done with. But I've never smacked a kid in my job. And I wouldn't, unless the parents made it very clear that that's what they want."

Be clear about what you want; let there be no room for misinterpretation. Let your care giver know what kinds of limit setting and punishment you want her to carry out. If you wouldn't spank your child, don't allow her to. Forbid punishment by force-feeding or food deprivation. And let her know that how your child is disciplined is one area in which you are unwilling to compromise. If her beliefs affect her ability to adhere to your wishes, then let her know the consequences.

CLEARING THE AIR

A friend of ours was in the midst of a cold war with her care giver, a woman who had been taking care of her son for almost two years. There was no communication at all; just a slow burn on the part of both the mother and the baby sitter of a two-year-old child. What was the problem? "She never comes in when I want her to," the mother said.

When questioned further, she expanded on her original statement. "I need her to come in at different times," she said. "I need her to be flexible." Had she spoken to the care giver about it? "I can't." As our discussion continued, it soon became clear that the mother would either have to fire the baby sitter or speak to her. She said she didn't know which would be more unpleasant. Then finally she relented and agreed to talk to her childcare worker.

The mother said she felt abused and abandoned; the care giver replied that she felt manipulated and exploited. It wasn't much, at best a little bit of headway. But at least the lines of communication had been opened a crack.

The mother spoke with us again; this time it became clear that on days when she didn't need the baby sitter, she didn't pay her. There was no set number of hours worked week to week, and no set weekly pay. It was suggested that there be a minimum weekly salary, not just an hourly wage. In addition, we felt that, whenever possible, the mother should plan her schedule far enough in advance so as to give at least a week's notice to the sitter about expected work hours.

The mother listened, and brought her proposals back to the baby sitter. A little more negotiation, a little more communication, and the problem was solved.

Be honest if something is bothering you, within limits. If a person is always ten minutes late to every play date, class, and activity and you get angry at her over and over again, it's no help. In this case, you might try changing the way you approach the situation, for example, you might write down all her appointments so that the care giver has a constant visual reminder of where she's supposed to be when.

Another limitation on honesty has to do with its effects on your

children. Psychologist Frances Bick describes the difference between expressing anger at a spouse and anger at a baby sitter, "You
can show anger at another family member because then your child
sees you talking calmly with or kissing daddy. There's an acceptable
resolution. With someone outside the family, it's different. You'd
never let your child know, for example, that you're angry at the
teacher. Kids don't get the whole story when you have an open
conflict with the childcare worker and it doesn't resolve to their
satisfaction."

Elaine Ruskin agrees. "Never say mommy is upset with the childcare person," she says. "Take it away from the person. Say,
'Mommy's upset because the house is a mess,' " not that you're
angry at the housekeeper for not doing her job.

WHEN PARENTS DISAGREE

One nanny said, "A friend in London left a job because the father
wanted to be strict and the mother was very loose. The kids were
four and six and their parents fought all the time about their upbringing. The kids laughed, they were disrespectful and angry. And
the nanny got caught in the middle because no matter how she
punished them it never pleased either parent."

One of the most awkward positions a childcare person can be
placed in is to be caught in a tug-of-war between warring parents.
In fact, numerous care givers told us that parents' power struggles
were among the principal reasons they and their friends left jobs.
One psychiatrist said that, in her experience, all too often husbands
who come home from work to find the house looking like a mess or
the kids misbehaving blame their wives for not handling the childcare person right. She says that this is but one of the many ways
parents try to bring childcare workers into the middle of their own
power struggles.

The experts agree: Work out your problems between yourselves. It's unfair to your childcare worker (not to mention your child) for you to carry your conflicts over into your relationships with children or the people you've hired to take care of them.

SAFETY AND SECURITY

Part of making it work is simply feeling secure in your care giver's ability to protect your child and to handle emergency situations. And part of the way you increase your sense of security is by talking about what might happen (and discussing appropriate responses) before anything does happen.

- Make it clear that your three-year-old should not cross the street riding his tricycle, that he should walk, holding hands with the baby sitter or another responsible adult.

- Make sure your small child cannot ingest poisons. That means laundry detergents should be placed out of reach at all times, by you and by your childcare person.

- Childproof your house, and insist that the baby sitter be vigilant in keeping it childproofed at all times. (For example, gates to stairways should always be closed when a toddler is in the house; if the baby sitter leaves the upstairs gate open when she goes downstairs—even for a minute—your child may try to follow.)

- Talk with your care giver about how to respond to an emergency—when to call you, when to call the pediatrician, and when to take action herself to deal with an acute medical emergency. You may also want to have her (as well as yourselves) attend a course on first aid, on child safety, or on child CPR (such as the popular BabyLife™ courses, as well as programs given in many metropolitan Ys by qualified professionals).

• Make sure she understands the basic rules of safety in public places: That she should never leave a small child unattended in a shopping center; that she should always be aware of where the child is in a playground; and that she should never leave a child alone in a car. Discuss talking to strangers with her. Let her know that nobody has the right to touch your child, that nobody needs to know her name and address, that she should never leave your child—even for a moment—with someone she does not know herself. And let her know your feelings about whether and when she may leave your child with other baby sitters.

In short, the best way to prevent your child from becoming a statistic is to take precautions in advance. And it's only common sense that any precaution you yourself take to protect your child should be taken by your care giver as well.

IN CASE OF EMERGENCY

We recommend that your care giver carry an index card, as well as change to make a phone call, at all times. Included on the card should be important phone numbers, along with information about both herself and the child. Here's the information that should be included on the card:

Child's name

Care giver's name

Child's address and phone number

Parents' names, work addresses, and phone numbers

Pediatrician's name, address, and phone number

Dentist's name, address, and phone number

Emergency numbers (poison control, ambulance service, 911)

Pharmacy address and phone number

Hospital (emergency room number)

Medical insurance number

Friends' and relatives' names and numbers (to call in emergency if parents can't be reached)

Taxi/car service numbers

There should be a similar list of phone numbers always located near the telephone in your home. Some people recommend that you also sign a statement authorizing your care giver to consent to emergency care for your child in your absence. This may, however, be unnecessary or redundant. For example, the New York State Public Health Law clearly states: "Medical, dental, health and hospital services may be rendered to persons of any age without the consent of a parent or legal guardian when, in the physician's judgment an emergency exists and the person is in immediate need of medical attention and an attempt to secure consent would result in delay of treatment which would increase the risk to the person's life or health."

For injuries or illnesses requiring treatment but that are not deemed emergencies, your care giver should always know where you are. If you're in a business meeting, she should be able to reach you when you check back into your office; if you're on vacation without your kids, she should have your itinerary (you can "fax" a consent even from the south of France, if necessary).

CHAPTER 7

When Childcare Needs Change

Life means change. That's a fact no one knows better than parents. From the moment your children are conceived (and in all likelihood until you've seen them off to college, to a job, to marriage—out of your home and into adulthood) your life is a continual torrent of changing needs and expectations.

- Expectant mothers may feel as though they'll never have their bodies to themselves ever again—but they do.

- Parents of newborn infants often believe they'll never get another unbroken night's sleep, but within a couple of months, baby is more than likely sleeping through the night—and so are the parents.

- Most babies sleep much of the day, and thus parents or care givers are likely to have lots of time to accomplish things around the house while the little one is asleep. But once baby starts to crawl, walk, run—in short, become a mobile toddler—the need for more constant supervision and attention (as well as the requirement for a grown-up who's mobile and energetic enough to keep up with a toddler's perpetual motion) presents itself.

- A two year old is a social being, and needs—besides all the attention—other children, other activities, and someone who can help him discover a wider world and learn the basics of acceptable social behavior.

- A preschool child needs someone who can (and will) read to him, as well as help him learn the basic skills of self-reliance (from dressing himself and brushing his own teeth to counting how many cookies he needs in order to give one to each friend at a get-together).

- A sibling arrives—the role of adults in a household becomes even more complex and challenging. Not only are there two (or three, or more) children to take care of physically, but there are also emotional needs to consider. It's not easy to be sensitive to each child, particularly when they're at different stages of development.

- A child goes to school; a mother or care giver is freed from hours of childcare for other activities. But after school, children still need someone to feed them, to make sure they do their homework, to supervise and direct their activities.

These are just some of the changes that virtually every household with children goes through; it may seem like a long list, but most parents know it's far from exhaustive.

And it doesn't even include the specifics of *your* household—changes in your economic status, in your housing situation, in the stability of your family life, in the thousands of other variables that exist in your family history. For example, you may find that you can afford to work part time, but that you can no longer afford or no longer need full-time childcare help; you may decide you want to spend more time with your child; you may get divorced, or remarried, or have another child; you or your spouse may lose a job or be transferred to another city; you may move from the city to the suburbs or vice versa. There are innumerable events, both large and small, that affect your decisions concerning childcare. The only constant is that they all necessitate some change in your childcare arrangement—whether in the "contract" you have with your current care giver or a change in care givers.

FINDING THE SOLUTION THAT WORKS FOR YOU

At every developmental stage, at every economic crossroad, at every new direction you or your child takes, you have alternative courses of action concerning childcare. You can change the written or unwritten contract with your childcare person by making adjustments in responsibilities, or even in basic terms of employment (such as hours and days worked or live-in/live-out arrangements). You can tear up the contract and create a brand new one. You can clear the slate and start again with a different care giver. You can maintain the status quo. No one way is right for every family (and no one solution is right for the same family every time), even in situations that on the surface seem virtually identical. The key is to find the solution that works for you—now.

Sometimes what's right for your family may be self-evident, but there are other times when it's quite difficult to gauge what's best. At times you may even feel uncomfortable with all your alternatives. Either because of guilt, or anger, or financial stress, or any number of other reasons, you may find yourself accepting as inevitable a solution that is really no solution at all. When you feel this way, it's best to step back and try to gain perspective; perhaps your first best course of action is to simply become aware of what's worked for other people when confronted with a similar quandary.

DEVELOPMENTAL CHANGES

One suburban New York mother asked us, "Do children need different kinds of relationships with care givers over time, or is stability the key factor?" The answers vary.

Some parents believe that no person (except for mommy and daddy) can possibly be right for a child at every developmental stage; others feel that continuity and a sense of being loved comes before specific appropriate skills. Some parents combine the two philosophies, at times making changes in personnel, at other times effecting changes in childcare responsibilities.

A Vermont child psychotherapist chose a stable relationship with a loving person as the best course for her child's needs. When her daughter was born she hired a baby nurse. She was very happy with the nurse, who was warm and showed genuine concern for her baby. She considered her alternatives, then asked the nurse to stay on as her daughter's permanent care giver. "Developmentally," she said, "I prefer that situation for my child—she only has to deal with one person and she seems extremely happy in this situation."

A single mother in Boston was concerned that her care giver could not give her children what they needed intellectually. Her children were two and four; the baby sitter was semiliterate. She wanted her kids to be encouraged in language development, and didn't see the care giver as being capable of helping them develop their skills. So she made a change, hiring someone who had skills she thought more appropriate to her children's developmental needs.

A New York advertising executive told us she believed in hiring new care givers periodically in order to accommodate her daughter's changing needs. When her baby was born, she employed a nurse/

care giver, a woman in her sixties who was very nurturing and slow paced. When her daughter was six months old, she replaced the nurse with a more energetic, younger woman, someone whom she felt could keep up with her now-mobile child; a year and a half later, she opted for someone who was highly literate and spoke perfect grammatical English (and who liked going to museums, concerts, and libraries). She was happy with her choices and felt that she was maximizing the potential benefits of childcare for her daughter.

While experts disagree about whether you should make childcare changes for developmental reasons, they generally do agree that changes should not be made cavalierly nor should they be made too frequently. Emotionally healthy children do become attached; a utilitarian fit-the-care-giver-into-the-developmental-slot kind of attitude can lead to the same lack of emotional connectedness that one mother evinced when she told us her feelings about the many people she had hired to take care of her children. "All those people," she said, "just come and go like background noise."

Psychologist Frances Bick told us, "If you change baby sitters often, kids may begin to think they're awful kids, that they're the reason the person is leaving. This may create a negative feeling about themselves, a feeling that makes it more difficult for them to ever have a relationship with anyone." Dr. Bick also says that the worst time to make a childcare change is between the ages of eighteen and twenty-six months; if it's at all possible, she suggests making changes before or after this period. The reason for this is that developmentally this period is most fraught with separation anxiety.

Child psychiatrist Dr. William Koch told us, "In one case, the mother changed the childcare person once a month, assuming— and hoping—that her child would not develop a relationship with the childcare people. That happened—with the end result that the child could not form a relationship with anyone."

SHOULD YOU CHANGE THE CONTRACT?

Obviously, as a child grows, the type of care he or she needs will change. If you find you have locked yourself into a rigid contract with your care giver (as to *exactly* what work she will do), you're bound to find your child's needs, and your own, being frustrated. So the question is not really whether to change the contract, it's how.

Recognizing that child development means constant change, Frances Bick states unequivocally, "The contract with your childcare person should be open-ended; every arrangement you make is temporary."

Changes in the contract may be simple adjustments to accommodate specific developmental changes, or they may encompass more general overhauls in responsibilities and work hours. One Washington, D.C., mother, who has thus far only made small changes, echoed Dr. Bick when she told us about her experiences. "I've employed three girls," she said, "all in their early twenties, and their responsibilities have all been relatively similar. Of course, as a child gets older you go less from being a play partner to being someone who arranges and supervises play dates. We've always left our 'contract' open-ended; the specifics of the job do change pretty often and with added responsibilities we've always given fair compensation."

Or, as Elaine Ruskin, consultant to the preschool programs at New York's West Side Y, says, "When you give a raise, you can change the rules."

Susan Kurnit, a teacher who works with care givers at the 92nd Street Y Parenting Center, has developed a perspective that balances the needs of everyone concerned—parents, children and childcare workers. "Very frequently changes need to be made in the household due to the child's growth," she says. "Childcare people often say that when the baby was three months old they had the time to cook and clean, but when the baby is seven months old they have no time, yet parents expect them to do the same housekeeping job.

"You can't expect the baby sitter to do all things. But it's hard for the childcare person to discuss this with you . . . imagine what would happen at your job if you told your boss you couldn't do something."

It's difficult for a childcare person—as your employee—to demand changes in the contract. But sometimes, if you're not aware of the pressures on her, you will find that either your child or your expectations suffer. If you demand that your house be spick-and-span, then the person who takes care of your active toddler will put her in a playpen in order to get the cleaning done. As your child grows, it's up to you to recognize that priorities change.

A doctor, who is the mother of a preschool child in New York, asked us, "How do you deal with increased free time as your child gets older and is at school? Is it reasonable for your baby sitter to do other work while your child is at school?" It's not unusual (nor is it unreasonable) to want to change the contract when your child starts nursery school. If you have a full-time childcare person, you may now want her to clean during the hours your child is in school. Susan Kurnit believes that you're perfectly within your rights to ask your care giver to expand her household responsibilities, but she warns that you shouldn't necessarily expect her to go along with your changes. "Childcare people see cleaning as a whole other area," she says.

"If you have a contract," declares Ms. Kurnit, "in which you explicitly state job duties, hours, etc.—perhaps the contract has to be gone over and revised periodically as your child's needs change."

When families have long-term relationships with care giver/ housekeepers, those periodic revisions in the contract are often what enables the arrangement to continue to work.

Eventually, many families find that they no longer need full-time care (either because the kids are in school or the moms are at home part-time), but they still need some in-home childcare. If they are happy with the performance of their full-time person, they often try to arrange a way to keep her. For example, some families try to create a split-week schedule for their childcare people, in which certain hours each day, or days each week, are spent in their homes, while the rest of the full-time work hours are spent in the home of another family that also has part-time childcare needs.

Others add different responsibilities (other than childcare) when the kids are in school or the parents are home, such as housework, shopping, sewing, laundry, even typing and filing. Still others cut hours and hope for the best. (Others cut hours but without a cut in pay.)

These changes don't always work out. They are all far from simple adjustments in the basic contract. But when they do work, they can help provide the stability many parents feel their children need.

One Washington, D.C., family, for example, which has employed the same person for ten years, told us its secret. The woman started when their first child was a baby; until all three of their children were in school, she did childcare exclusively while another person came in to clean. When the kids were all in school, she started to clean. And as they got bigger and needed less physical care, she began to cook as well. The time she arrives at work has become less and less important—now the parents' principal concern is that her work (running the household) gets done and that she is there when the younger children get home from school. Recently the family changed more of the fundamental terms of the contract: She now works three afternoons and one full day for them and the rest of her work time is spent with another family in the neighborhood.

A New York couple, whose son recently started a full-day school program, felt "we did not want him to lose the stability and security of this positive and loving four-year relationship." They felt they could change the specifics of the work done by the care giver; they did not feel they could change the hours. Now, while the boy is in school, the care giver/housekeeper is doing housework and errands.

A Philadelphia mother of two small children went in the exact opposite direction. She had bad experiences with two baby sitters, both of whom she fired for cause. Then she found someone with whom she was happy. The woman was responsible and flexible as to her hours and days of work (which was an important consideration for the mother). But the mother was very reluctant to make a change in the care giver's responsibilities. "Although she'd probably react well," said the mother, "she's an older woman, and I don't think she can take on much that is new at this point." For her, not seeking a change in her childcare person's job description was a decision, based in part on her previous experiences and in part on her perception of the woman's limitations.

Sometimes, rather than really thinking about their options, parents back their way into a decision. Although it may be in their interest to have their care givers take on added responsibilities, they simply don't ask. Why not? Some of the responses were, "I'm afraid she'll say no," "it would be unfair with her wages," "I want her to concentrate on childcare," "I can't afford to pay her more," and "I don't think she's capable."

Very often, this reluctance to ask leads parents into a cul-de-sac. Many feel compelled to hire someone new—with a different job description—rather than attempting to change the contract of a person whose work is satisfactory. For those who feel the care giver is incapable of doing the job differently, or who feel they can't afford to pay more (and that the new responsibilities necessarily entail a higher wage), this position makes some sense. But if you're happy with your childcare worker's job performance and money is not a factor, then not asking is more of an emotional than a practical method of dealing with your needs.

One New York family told us about their success in changing the contract as their needs change. The mother, who spoke with us about her childcare history, works part time (and has had a similar work schedule through most of her children's lives); her husband is a full-time working professional.

"We had a baby nurse when our daughter was born, and she stayed for a while—several months—but then she just wasn't right. Good for an infant but not for a growing baby. So we let her go and then we hired Martha.

"Martha has worked for us for ten years. She's an older woman, very grandmotherly, and there's a lot of love between her and the kids. When she started her hours were 8:30 to 5:30, and we had to adjust our workdays in order to accommodate that schedule. But it worked out fine. And of course her duties—both with our daughter and with our son after he was born—were principally childcare. From the beginning we made it clear that childcare was the first priority and housework came second.

"But as the kids got older we needed a different arrangement. During the hours when the kids are in school there's not much childcare to do—and now that my son's eight and my daughter's eleven, they're pretty independent in general.

"Now when they're at school Martha works from 1:00 to 6:00 (I like someone in the house all afternoon), and when they're home I still have her come in all day. Her hours are very flexible.

"Even though she works less hours now, I've never decreased her salary. It's important for me to know that she's there when I need her.

"Incidentally, she was reluctant to change the arrangement at first but I stressed that her salary wouldn't change; now she enjoys her new hours and is more than amenable to doing new things in the house—that way she won't get bored—she even cooks dinner for us four nights a week. But I haven't asked her to do 'heavy' housekeeping. It's a delicate balance.

"I think the most important thing when someone takes care of your children is that she loves and cares for them and is responsible for their safekeeping.

"Why have we been together for ten years? She respects me and I respect her."

SIBLING ARRIVAL

When a household with one child welcomes a second, the household (and everyone in it) changes along with the new arrival. The older sibling may not be completely ecstatic about giving up his position at the center of the universe; the parents may find that they're both exhausted and in an emotional tug-of-war between their children; the care giver may feel similarly torn, or she may feel as though the contract has been breached. With the arrival of a sibling, a new childcare contract is definitely in order.

One Boston couple with a three-year-old daughter believed their son's birth necessitated only minor adjustments. They offered their childcare worker a 5 percent raise to go along with her increased responsibilities. The care giver was still expected to do the light cleaning and general errands; she was still expected to pick up the older child from her nursery program, feed her lunch, and take her to afternoon activities such as play dates and the playground; and in addition, she was expected to provide primary care for the little girl's infant brother. The care giver felt the parents were asking too much and giving too little.

A struggle ensued between the parents and the care giver. The care giver asked for a 25 percent raise; the parents replied that her demand was ridiculous. Their compromise was to decrease her household responsibilities minimally and raise their pay offer to 10 percent. There was an uncomfortable standoff.

Then the baby sitter was out sick for two days and the mother was forced to stay home alone with her two children. She was literally overwhelmed; when one child wasn't demanding attention, the other one was. She couldn't mop the floors; she barely had time to do the dishes.

When the caregiver returned to work, the parents presented a new proposal: They offered a 15 percent raise now, another 5 percent in six months; they decreased her household responsibilities and hired someone else to clean their house one day a week; they accepted that the job was a lot bigger now than it was before. The childcare worker accepted the parents' proposal, and peace was restored.

It's both fair and prudent to couple a significant raise with the increased responsibilities of taking care of a second child in a household. In fact, if you can afford it, it's almost a necessity to keep the peace.

If, rather than rethinking the contract and salary of your old childcare person, you're considering changing care givers after the birth of a new baby, think again about your older child's needs. Her life is already being disrupted by the new arrival. If you change care givers at this time without a very good reason, you're giving her a very clear message—that her feelings and needs are no longer important to you. For that reason alone, it's best not to change care givers at this time.

After the arrival of a new baby, it's unreasonable to assume that your care giver will be able to do the same amount of housework she did before the drastic increase in her childcare duties. As one New Jersey mother said, "Our baby sitter used to do more housework, but that was when we had only one child. Now with two, her duties are closer to full-time childcare."

But even a raise, or an adjustment in your expectations for a clean house, doesn't always work. Fretta Reitzes, director of the Parenting Center at the 92nd Street Y, says there are other issues involved as well as money and formal duties. For example, can your care giver adjust to the change emotionally? Okay, she was hired to take care of one child, but now here comes another. How will she handle the sibling rivalry, will she play favorites (this is a particular problem if she's become really attached to the first child), does she feel more comfortable with a child of one sex than with the other, and will she be able to navigate the increased complexity of the relationships in a larger family? The inability to satisfactorily answer any of these questions may make increased compensation and formal respon- sibilities unimportant considerations; if your children are not get- ting the care they need (emotional as well as physical) you may have to change more than the contract, you may have to change the care giver.

When a new baby arrives, many parents also find that changes need to be made in the type of childcare arrangement they have. The type and hours of childcare coverage you had before now may no longer be enough.

One mother we interviewed who had a baby daughter and was free-lancing at home found that a college student, working part time in her home, fit her needs quite well. But with the birth of her second child, her needs changed.

With everything she had to do, her life became a juggling act. She was working three days a week, five or six hours a day. She had a young child who needed attention and she had a baby. It was just too much.

A college student no longer fit the bill. The mother couldn't afford to have a care giver who would be unable to come in during exams, or who left for a week's vacation at semester break. She needed someone more mature, stable, and reliable.

At first she wanted to hire someone three full days a week (to coincide with her own work schedule), but it was very difficult to find a person who both fit her requirements and was willing to work the hours she specified. Perhaps it was partially a result of her difficulty in finding the right part-time person, but she soon real- ized she needed full-time help, both for childcare and to take care of general household chores, which had increased considerably with the birth of her second child. She realized that to feel comfortable about her children's well-being and the state of her household, she would have to spend the money necessary to hire a full-time professional baby sitter/housekeeper, a person who was capable and mature enough to accept the full range of responsibilities the job now entailed.

A professional woman, divorced and the mother of three, told us about her history with in-home childcare. Her story is indicative of how many different ways your life as a family can change and how important it is to make almost continual adjustments to changed circumstances.

"One thing I've found is that, as my children grew, they needed new childcare people. The first lady we had was warm and loving, she sang beautiful lullabies . . . she was great with a baby. But she would have been terrible helping with homework and organizing play dates. She was a friend of my mother's, a sixty-five-year-old Irish woman. She couldn't keep up with a child. And after eight months, once my baby was crawling, she told me she couldn't handle it.

"Then I had a Colombian woman. She lived with us for two years. She was warm and loving too . . . but when I told her I was pregnant, she said she didn't want to take care of more than one child. It's a good thing she left too, because I had twins, and she really couldn't have handled them.

"The next person also stayed about two years . . . through my divorce. Then I found out she was giving information to my husband. First I told her to stop; then when I found she was still doing it—*and* doing his laundry—I fired her. I told her I needed someone different, gave her two weeks' pay and asked her to leave.

"She came back a few times to see the children—which was fine—but I really didn't want her around anymore. You don't need a spy in your home.

"Now I have an English woman. She's thirty, she's been with us for three and a half years, and I'm sponsoring her for her green card. It's the only kind of work she's ever done.

"I pay her $275 a week gross and take out Social Security and taxes. She lives in and works Monday through Friday 7:00 A.M. to 6:00 P.M. She used to go out a lot at night (she talks a lot to me about her boyfriend) but I told her she has to be available Monday, Wednesday, and Thursday nights, in case I have to work late. Tuesday nights and weekends are her time off. I also have someone come in once a week to clean.

"It's not a bed of roses, but she listens . . . and generally responds. For example, I had to explain to her that my older son is jealous of the twins. They have each other to play with. So he's at a disadvantage.

"The baby sitter had just not thought about what was going on with my son. She thought he was being bad and was sending him to his room, which only reinforced his resentment. I explained what I thought was going on, and urged her to allow—no, to encourage and help arrange—for his friends to come over and play.

"The children are quite attached to their baby sitter, but she's not a parent. Sometimes she's almost like another child to me. To make it work, I believe you've got to have a process of ongoing communication and intervention. I don't want to abdicate my position in the household; I want my presence to be felt."

YOUR RESPONSIBILITIES TO YOUR CARE GIVER

You're moving, perhaps to a different neighborhood, or from the city to the suburbs, or to another part of the country. You've had a good relationship with your baby sitter. She's been loyal, helpful—a good employee. She's a person your children love. But now everything's different.

When you have live-out childcare help and you move to a different neighborhood, travel time is a principal consideration. If it took her twenty minutes to get to work before, and now she's an hour and a half away, it may be unfeasible for her to make the move with you.

If you move from the city to the suburbs, it's often too difficult or too expensive for a city dweller to commute. (Because of the problems with commuting care givers, many suburban families find that, where they once employed childcare people who lived on their own, they now need live-in help.) If your baby sitter isn't able to make the move with you, you'll most likely start looking for alternatives. And if you're moving out of the area, it's almost a certainty that you won't be taking her with you. It's time to say goodbye.

Moving isn't the only major change that dictates a reassessment of your childcare situation. Divorce, a change in your job situation, and the kids growing up—all mean significant adjustments. If the situation requires less than a total break, you may opt for time-sharing or ask her to do more heavy cleaning (or even typing). If termination is your only choice, and your relationship with her has been a good one, what are your responsibilities to her? Feeling sorry that you have to let her go is not enough.

You may have to let her go, but you don't have to leave her in the lurch. You can actively help her get another job, provide her with severance pay or support her filing for unemployment compensation.

One family we interviewed, who had relocated from the city to the suburbs after employing the same live-out care giver for over five years, found that, once they moved, they had to hire a live-in person. They gave their old employee $1,000 in severance pay and extended her healthcare benefits (which they had been paying) for another six months. There are any number of things you can do that will help your childcare worker financially after you're gone. Just because she's no longer working for you doesn't mean she no longer exists.

HER NEEDS CHANGE

Your family's needs change, and so do those of your care giver. She may have problems in her own home; you will have to decide how flexible you can be to accommodate her. She may get pregnant; if she wants to continue working for you, you'll have to decide whether it's feasible (you'll need at least a temporary replacement). She may be ill, or have immigration problems, or want to go to school, or fall in love. So many possibilities—and many of them require *you* to make decisions. When her needs change, your big decision is how flexible you want to be.

A number of parents we've spoken with have hired temporary baby sitters when their regular people gave birth or had to leave for an extended period to deal with immigration problems. This is a situation that is inherently stressful, for various reasons. One is simply the problems of adjustment for your children—getting used to a new person, then (often just when they've begun feeling comfortable) having that new person leave when the old one comes back. Parents also often resent the extra burdens placed on them— of training someone and holding open a job. And we were told of one instance where the care giver found her own temporary replacement, whom the family actually liked better than their original person. When the original care giver was ready to come back, the family faced a dilemma about what to do. After some soul-searching, they finally decided to take their old childcare person back, even though the family would have preferred another solution. The parents felt they had made an agreement with both people that was as inviolable as any contract, that to keep the replacement would be unfair to the first person and that it would also send a message to the new person that they were not people who could be trusted to keep their promises. Other families, of course, make other decisions, but for these people, considerations of fairness and ethics came ahead of their own interests.

Many parents with live-in help find that when their childcare people get their green cards (and are thus able to work legally), they no longer want to live in. These workers see greater opportunities opening up for them with their newfound legal status (and who can blame them); for the first time they've been freed to join the general labor force. They see the possibility of higher pay and social security and unemployment insurance coverage.

It's not unusual, nor is it unreasonable, for a care giver, no matter her length of service or the employing family's "kindness," to leave a sixty- to seventy-hour-a-week job, a job in which she's always on call, a job that amounts to two or three dollars an hour in pay for actual hours worked. Yet many parents who employ childcare workers in such conditions are shocked when their employees come back from getting their labor certification and quit. It shouldn't be such a shock.

Childcare workers' personal relationships also frequently cause strain in their relationship to a household. Perhaps the childcare worker left her own children back in her home country; she misses them, and gradually becomes more and more depressed and homesick. It's a classic case of displacement, frequently cited as one of the principal problems an immigrant has in adjusting. It's a situation that may not have a solution. Yet you still have to deal with its effects on your household.

Another scenario we've heard about quite frequently was well-stated by one Chicago mother. "My childcare person," she said, "a twenty-two-year-old Irish girl, came here to work for us about six months ago. She's illegal. She's terrific, and we're very happy with her, and that's the first time ever—we had three baby sitters before her and fired them all. Maureen met a guy not long after she got here, and the relationship with him seems to give her stability emotionally. But she wants to see him as often as possible, so whereas she was willing to work virtually any evening we asked when she first got here, now she has demanded Wednesday night off—from 7:00 P.M. until 9:00 the next morning, as well as every weekend from 7:00 P.M. until Monday morning. Because we like her, we've accommodated her. Now we make other baby-sitting arrangements if we want to go out on weekends."

Sometimes a baby sitter's outside relationships have more of an effect on her relationship with her employers than simply adjusting their weekend arrangements. One live-in care giver from Germany we spoke with has worked with the same family for almost two years; they are sponsoring her for legal immigration status (even paying her lawyer's fees); she is taking college courses at night; they installed a cable television in her room and pay part of her medical insurance. They've allowed girlfriends of hers to stay with her for periods up to six weeks and have allowed her parents to stay with her when they were on vacation in America. But the sitter recently met a man and, she says, "I suddenly found myself restricted by rules we had never spoken about."

He came to visit her during work hours, and although she says he was very loving toward the children, the parents told her not to have him visit while she was working. "Then he stayed too late in the evening," the sitter told us, "and he was staying for dinner and he was there when they had guests and they asked me to stop all of that.

"They want me to live here," she said, "but I feel like they have a hold on my life. I feel restricted in my time after work—when he visits me in my room after work hours his presence seems to bother them. I've never asked him to stay over; I think it would create bad feelings. And I haven't talked to them about it because I don't want to poison the atmosphere. I just felt I had freedom and now I have rules. I guess that's part of the business."

If you were the employers of this young woman, what would you do? How would you respond to the changes in the personal life of your baby sitter? It seems that a good part of the bad feelings is the result of a mutual misunderstanding of the limits. But you can't always foresee changes, and you can't set every possible guideline at the beginning of a care giver's employment.

In many cases, you simply have to deal with changes as they occur and make decisions within your own ethical framework based on what is in your best interests and those of your children. After all, you have employed a person to fulfill a specific job. If the job isn't being done to your satisfaction, or if your needs and expectations change and you feel the care giver cannot meet your new requirements, you have to make a change. What this change is varies; sometimes you can negotiate compromises with your care giver (see chapter 6), but sometimes compromise is not possible and you have to look elsewhere for a solution.

CHAPTER 8

If It's Not Working

Life with baby sitter isn't always sweet-smelling flowers—sometimes the bed of roses is filled with thorns. In fact, if your children grow up and you never have childcare problems, you can count yourselves among the fortunate few. At some time during the childcare years most of us have problems—personality conflicts, money conflicts, philosophical conflicts, gnawing dissatisfactions that can blossom into destructive weeds—causing the relationship between family and care giver to become strained, or even break down altogether. What can go wrong between your family and your care giver?

Sometimes the trade-offs you've been making simply stop working, "I'm not altogether satisfied with her energy level but she's very loving toward my daughter," gradually becomes "She's slow as molasses and it drives me crazy"; "I wish her language skills were better but she's very responsible and warm," is suddenly transformed into "I want my son to learn how to read and she's not helping at all." In that case, the scales have simply tipped; you've reached a point where what was once predominantly positive is now predominantly negative. It happens.

When things don't work out it's often because a family has hired the wrong person, they have misconceptions about who they're hiring, they don't check references, and they assume too much and know too little. When this happens people usually know relatively early on (generally even before the end of the trial period). The principal recourse is simple—start over.

There may be a breakdown in communication, a lack of trust, a personality conflict, or a difference in philosophy. Any of these things may occur at any time, but they're not inevitable. Keeping the lines of communication open may prevent a loss of trust; talking on a regular basis about your child's development may help strengthen the bonds between your baby sitter and your family, letting her know what you want may serve as a guide to her. Susan Kurnit of New York's 92nd Street Y Parenting Center believes it generally takes one to one and a half years for the resentment to build up to a point that's untenable, *unless you talk about it.*

WHEN SHE TAKES HER TROUBLES TO WORK

Problems also arise from instability in the care giver's life. If your au pair is involved in a tempestuous love affair, you can almost bet her problems will spill over into her relationship with your family. If your care giver has her own small children, she may feel torn between your family and hers. She may feel that she's neglecting her own kids for yours. And she may resent it.

One Brooklyn couple was drawn, slowly but inexorably, into the marital problems of their baby sitter. There were times she didn't show up for work, other times she begged them for help in protecting her from her alcoholic husband, times when she and her husband were reconciled and she asked them to help him find work, still other times when she herself came to work battered and exhausted. Their natural sympathy for her plight took them deeper and deeper into the morass of her relationship with her husband. Besides, they reasoned, she was very attached to their children and was loving and warm to them. But the destructiveness of the woman's marriage wore everyone down, and the children suffered some neglect as a result of it. And in the more than two years the situation went on, it never resolved itself. It never really got better, and finally the woman's problems caused such a breakdown in her ability to carry out her job that the parents asked her to leave.

If you've hired an undocumented foreign worker, you may be asking for a situation in which she leaves on a vacation and doesn't come back. She may go home to her native country, or get a green card and set out for greener pastures, or just find another job (although that could happen with anybody). A person with roots—family and community ties—in your own area is less likely to be transient.

WHO'S WORKING FOR WHOM?

A Connecticut mother told us this story. "We had an au pair who was a very nice, thoughtful, warm, and loving person. She took evening college classes and worked elsewhere on weekends. With all her outside activities, there was a point at which she was really not doing what we needed or expected. I wrote out exactly what her duties were and discussed them with her. I gave her many verbal warnings—she was not defensive, she just changed the subject. She was really no help to us at all. I finally asked her to move out with two weeks' notice. I don't think she ever really understood and I think she felt bitter about it. If I had to do it again I wouldn't drag out so long; I'd just get it over with."

Even if your care giver lives in your home, she is there to work for you. If she acts as though her life comes first, even during the hours you need her, then you really don't need her—you need someone else.

ILLUSIONS AND COLLUSION

Your childcare person's relationships with your family are not limited to the children. She interacts with mothers, fathers, grandparents, and older siblings as well. And in the course of these individual interactions, there are times when the baby sitter has the opportunity to play the parents off against one another or to take the child into collusion—in short, to manipulate the individual members of the family in order to get what she wants.

Psychiatrists warn about childcare workers who invite children into collusion; for example, if you have a no smoking rule in your household and she smokes, she may tell your six-year-old child, "Don't tell your mom; this will be our secret." In this kind of situation, the child is forced to choose between Mommy and the mommy substitute. It's a difficult choice, one that is guilt and fear inducing whatever the child does. And if the collusion is more than implicit (as in the example above), it can be even more of a problem for a child.

Care givers also often play parents off against one another. This is unacceptable, although at times understandable, behavior when it comes from your child. But when it comes from one of your child's role models, it is intolerable. What do we mean by playing the parents off against one another? It could be testing limits, going from one to the other when a request is denied; choosing the easy one to talk to when asking for a day off or a raise; showing respect for one parent and ignoring the other; becoming intimate and personal with the mother when the father is angry; exploiting a couple's marital problems; complaining about the mother's restrictiveness to the father. One mother told us she fired someone who "never did what I wanted and was nice only to my husband." Many parents spoke with us about the disparate ways their care givers responded to them and to their spouses. And of course there's the old bugaboo (which occasionally even happens in real life) of the au pair running off with the husband.

Sometimes childcare people project an illusion of indispensability. A person who does this would like you to feel that your home would fall apart without her. No matter how competent and skilled a person is, this is a dangerous misperception, one that can be more crippling than constructive to you and to your child's growth. It can polarize your family, and can make you feel trapped—as though any other arrangement is not feasible. The fact is, no one person (with the exception of a parent) is indispensable to your child's well-being.

WHOSE HOME (CHILD) IS IT ANYWAY?

A musician couple in Toronto told us about a nanny they employed for a year before letting her go recently. "I like to spend the time that I'm home being with, and taking care of, my daughter," said the mother. This was difficult for the nanny, who seemed to require a lot of control. "She was accustomed to doing things in a certain way, and was not able to be flexible or feel comfortable doing otherwise. She was gradually taking over the household duties (shopping, cooking, etc.) and I was feeling more and more like a guest in my own home. I'm sure her intentions were good, but I had to explain that I preferred to do some of these things myself." But people who require control often have trouble giving it up. "Soon after that," continued the Toronto mother, "she had been working for us about six months, she took a sudden apparent dislike to us and to our child. She became unfriendly toward us and impatient with our daughter. She never told us why. The reasons she put forward (not enough work and the difference in our household routine from her parents' home) were not substantial enough to justify her behavior. Without informing us, she sought and accepted another job, then told us she was leaving us in a month. The situation was so tense it was untenable. After a week I made alternate arrangements and told her she was free to go."

You, the parents, are the people who make the decisions about what's best for your child. You are the responsible parties. If you allow another person, no matter how "qualified" she is, to decide the way you run your household, or especially the way you bring up your child, you are being irresponsible.

One mother, faced with a childcare worker's "inappropriately restrictive treatment of my son," took decisive action. It was respectfully explained to the woman, who was in her mid-sixties, that with the difference in child-rearing philosophies between herself and the parents, it wouldn't work out. She was given two weeks' severance pay (and was herself relieved, feeling that she was too old for the job), and the little boy "got better care" when the family hired someone new.

We were told of another instance in which the care giver, who was a stickler for "good behavior," overstepped her bounds when she forced an eight-year-old girl, who was running a high fever, to clear the table for herself and her sister after dinner. In the view of the parents, the baby sitter's insistence on following the rules broke a cardinal rule—that of taking care of their children's well-being.

BABY SITTER BURNOUT

Many parents and experts have spoken with us about "baby sitter burnout." One mother defined the term as "the point where the job is drudgery; when the baby sitter hates doing the job and wants to get out."

Remember, she's working in someone else's home, taking care of someone else's child in a way prescribed by other people. She is not a free agent, she is probably not particularly well paid, and her job— although important—has very low status in the outside world. Never mind that she's loving, warm, supportive; never mind that she's become attached to the child (she knows that the attachment is almost certainly temporary); never mind that she's doing a terrific job helping someone grow. There's a time when, for her, all the negative aspects of the job—the boredom, the low social and economic status, the inevitability of separation—may well outweigh the positive aspects of even the best childcare situation.

Some baby sitters change jobs; some change professions. Some employers find their solution in changing sitters every year or two; others tell us that, by increasing the job's responsibilities and challenges, they have alleviated the boredom their care givers felt after an extended period with their families.

PROBLEM-PRONE PARENTS

Some families are prone to problems: They hire people who are incompetent or inappropriate, then wonder why things don't work out; or they themselves are so hard to get along with (or their attitudes are so negative) that even the most understanding and wonderful care givers feel abused; or the relationship between family members is strained. Whatever the reasons, when a family's childcare arrangements fail to work out again and again, the problem is very often inside the family itself. Sometimes it's just a matter of luck. Most people have had negative experiences at one time or another. But if you have a pattern with your childcare workers that is disastrous, there's more than likely something besides luck at work.

One family we know of, in which the father, who is much older than the mother, is both stricter with his son and jealous of the time the child spends with his mother, has had a succession of over a dozen full-time people in less than three years. The conflicts that rage through this family have spilled over on their childcare workers; the mother wants an ally in her struggles with her husband; the son is prone to acting-out behavior; the father insists on discipline and propriety from his employees—it all adds up to an untenable situation for a care giver.

Psychologists warn about parents giving childcare people mixed messages, saying that when the father says one thing and the mother says another, the help is inevitably caught in the middle. Parents must be consistent in their directions to a care giver. She should not be the battleground on which the parents' philosophical (or marital) battles are fought.

Sometimes the problem with your care giver stems from your responses to your children's behavior. If you see your child manipulating, or bossing his care giver around and you don't like what you see, you may blame the baby sitter for her passivity and fire her. But if you see a repetition of the problem, you may be looking in the wrong place for what went wrong. Perhaps you've given your child the message that he is superior and can do what he wants, or given the childcare person the message that her job is to be at your child's beck and call. If you see the same problem again and again, maybe it's time to take a critical look inside your own family for the source of the problem, and take the actions necessary to correct it.

A family is a hierarchy, with you, the parents, as the ultimate authorities. Your care giver is your surrogate; that means when you are not around she is the authority. When you undermine that authority, you teach your child disrespect. It's best to keep your problems with your care giver away from your child. Of course you want to know your child's feelings about his childcare, whether he's happy and contented and well taken care of, but don't share your conclusions with him. If you think your care giver is not particularly intelligent or attractive—keep those opinions among yourselves.

Because when you do something to undermine your child's respect for his care giver, when you undermine her authority, you're also undermining your child's sense of order and well-being. He needs the security of feeling he's taken care of by someone who is worthy of respect.

WHY IT'S NOT WORKING—
CARE GIVERS' VIEWS

One of the questions we asked childcare workers in our interviews and questionnaires had to do with what made a job situation not work *for them*. Along with the expected answers of "They treated me like a slave," "They expected me to work all the time and thought they were being generous when they gave me their old clothes," and "They didn't pay me enough to live," came a series of answers about the job and relationships with family members.

A great many care givers cited the marital problems of the parents as being a principal cause of their leaving their jobs; they felt trapped in the middle of a no-win situation. Although several said they sympathized with the children, they found themselves unable to tolerate the tension between the parents and left the job.

Other childcare workers told us they quit because of conflicts between the parents about bringing up baby. Some complained that the parents were never home, creating a situation that included long hours and, in many instances even more critical, in which they were basically being asked to act as the children's mothers (albeit without any real authority).

On the other hand, several care givers told us of their problems with mothers who hovered, constantly supervising and criticizing what they were doing. In reaction, one went so far as to say, "I'll never work for a nonworking mother again."

Another frequent complaint was that parents discounted, or simply did not listen to, what care givers had to say about the children. One British nanny who said, "a good care giver will have genuine concern for a child" also told us of two instances in which parents ignored her requests concerning the safety of their children. "I knew George's car seat was not safe and I asked the father to get another, which he would have had to do soon because George had outgrown the other. The father refused. I felt I could not in good conscience continue to function in a situation where I was being ignored, and where I was not being allowed to do my job."

"In Byron's family," she continued, "I told the parents to put slabs over the stove to ensure that the child wouldn't put his fingers on the burners. The father didn't take me seriously. But finally, after I asked several times, they took care of it."

Care givers have legitimate gripes, and their independent observations about your household and children often have a great deal of merit. You'd do well to listen if you want to maximize a good care giver's effectiveness. If you don't listen, if you don't take her seriously, you may soon be looking for someone new.

ALTERNATIVE COURSES OF ACTION

When things aren't working, you have various ways to improve the situation. A breakdown in communication or a developing personality conflict can often be remedied by talking about it. Tell her what you want, clear the air, see if she responds. Conflicts can often be resolved by simply making positions clear.

One mother told us, "I had an au pair one summer and it made me furious that every morning she would make a fruit salad for herself and never offer any to anyone." She confronted the au pair with her selfishness; the au pair innocently responded that she didn't realize anyone else wanted any. It was reasonable for the mother to assume that the au pair was being selfish, but it just wasn't true. After that, she always offered to make fruit salad for everyone.

If there is a specific conflict causing bad feelings (such as a dispute over hours, salary, or duties), compromise is not out of the question. For example, you want her to work until 7:00, but she wants to leave at 6:00—if in other respects you like her and you are able to get home in time, why not try a 6:30 compromise?

Sometimes you have to literally "lay down the law." If you're not getting what you want, you may have to ask for it in no uncertain terms. Tell her, "No television"; let her know you want the baby's laundry done and let her know the consequences if she doesn't do what you ask.

And then there are those occasions when you have no alternative, and there is no way of improving the situation. In those cases—whether they're the result of insubordination, theft, incompetence, alcohol or drug abuse, poor care, or worse—talking about it, compromising, or giving her one more chance may just make a bad situation worse. Your only choice may be to fire her.

REASONS FOR DISMISSAL

Everyone has his or her own level of tolerance. Some people can live with uncomfortable feelings, others can't. Some can wink their eyes at a bending of the rules, others are stricter. You'll have to decide what your own limits are. Obviously, in situations that involve your children's physical safety and emotional well-being, there can be no compromises. But the resolutions to many other problems are as dependent on your personal style (and the thickness of your skin) as they are on objective factors.

Maybe you'll sail through the childcare years with no serious problems between your family and your care giver. If you're lucky, your limits will never be tested. But many families are not so lucky.

The point at which a conflict or a problem with the care your child is receiving becomes irresolvable is often subjective. You have to decide for yourself—in many cases, instantaneously. The following are some problems that can lead to dismissal.

- *You and your care giver may be incompatible, like oil and water.* You may have no specific cause for dismissal, just that you don't like or don't trust her. Your conceptions of the job may not coincide. She may be ineffectual or domineering. You might find her emotionally unstable, intrinsically unsuited for childcare, or she may even remind you of your mother-in-law. One mother told us, "When you feel instinctively that it's not going to work, that's the time to bail out." If you want to fire her, it's your right.

- *She may be insubordinate, refusing to take direction on her conduct in the job.* Perhaps you told her you don't want your children playing outside when it's 101 degrees in the shade, but she took them out anyway. Or you let her know you don't want your kids drinking soft drinks, but it slips out that she gives them a cola drink every day with lunch. She may argue with you (which is different from giving her opinion), refuse to do what you ask, break the rules that you've set up for your household, lie to you about her activities, or be openly disrespectful. Insubordination is a perfectly legitimate cause for dismissal.

- *Your children may not like her.* Whatever the reason, if they are uncomfortable, you must listen to them. Their lives are the ones most affected by the care giver. Who are you going to believe if your child tells you something happened and the care giver denies it? Some kids lie, of course, but as a parent, you have to believe your child unless there's incontrovertible evidence to the

contrary. (Or it may trouble you that she doesn't get along with
their friends' nannies. Although she may have a good reason for
not liking the other care givers in the neighborhood, the effect is
still negative—your children are being deprived of their social
lives.)

• *Your networking system—the mothers in the playground, the neigh-*
bors, your friends, and your friends' care givers—may report to you
that she's not taking good care of your child. Take these types of
report seriously, particularly if you hear them repeatedly; they
may well be valid.

• *She may drink, or steal, or take drugs.* You may feel like you want to
give her another chance, but your better judgment tells you that
you don't want to take a chance on coming home with your
house gone—or worse yet, with your child hurt by a care giver
whose judgment is impaired by alcohol or drugs. One mother,
who told us she came home to find remnants of marijuana
cigarettes in her ashtray, fired the care giver on the spot. How
many chances do you want to take with your child's well-being?

ABUSE AND NEGLECT

A friend of a friend overheard a conversation between baby sitters in
the playground. While the toddlers in their care played, the care
givers all talked about their problems getting the children to take
their naps—all except one. She was heard to say, "I have no problem. I just give him a little nip and he naps."

Our friend's friend called the mother of the child in this woman's
care; she didn't know her, but she felt she had to say something.
What she found out was that the child was having learning and
developmental problems, that he often seemed confused and tired,

and that the parents had taken him to his pediatrician concerning these problems. They had no idea of the cause.

What parents haven't worried, at one time or another, about their children's safety? What parents haven't been concerned, leaving a child alone with a baby sitter, a teacher, even a relative, due to the prevalence of child abuse in our society? Pediatrician Dr. Judy Goldstein says, "Child abuse is the biggest concern on the part of parents, bar none."

There is no punishment that can bring a damaged child back to health, or that can erase the scars of physical, sexual, or mental abuse or neglect. And there is no issue more important to you than protecting your child from abuse.

If you have any doubts about sexual or physical abuse, call your pediatrician immediately. If you have any question that a care giver is in any way abusing your child, under no circumstances should you ever leave that person alone with your child again.

If a child is abused even once it can be traumatic to the child. Some people say the incident has to be catastrophic to have permanent effects, but studies show that kids suffer, even if there's been only *one* incident.

If you were careful in hiring; if you thoroughly checked references, watched your care giver interact with your child, spoke with her about her background and philosophy—if you did all these things then you're probably relatively secure in the feeling that your child is free from the danger of abuse. If, during the training period, you spoke frequently with your childcare worker, observed her with your child (and took note of your child's responses), and clarified your own feelings about discipline (an acceptable form of punishment for one person may be totally unacceptable to another; if you are opposed to spanking you must make your feelings, and your recourse in case of transgression, crystal clear), then you may feel even more secure. If you have continued to keep an open line of communication with your sitter even after the training period, if you've kept your ears and your eyes open, you are justified in feeling almost certain that your child is not being abused or neglected. But you should never close your eyes to what's happening when you're not around—see no evil, hear no evil, speak no evil doesn't work when it comes to protecting your child from abuse and neglect.

WARNING SIGNS OF ABUSE AND NEGLECT

One of the most frightening things about child abuse is that it can happen to anyone. Never discount this problem, never feel that your child is immune. You can never feel so secure that you can stop being vigilant and observant of what's going on with your child. Although your child is probably safe, you can't take it for granted, because in the end what's at stake is your child's life and well-being.

Child psychiatrist Dr. Jack Snyder has much to tell parents about the telltale signs of abuse and neglect. He says the most common age for physical abuse is infancy and early toddlerhood. This is partially because it's an age when the child requires the most care— and particularly with a toddler, it's a period when a child may become especially rebellious and hard to handle. (Anyone who's tried to change a diaper on a struggling two-year-old knows this is the truth.) In addition, an infant is unable to speak, and a toddler is just learning the use of language. Thus, an abuser may feel as though there's no way he or she can be caught.

Even with an older child, the silence is often difficult to break down. This is usually the result of fear. Sometimes a child will tell his parents something such as, "My baby sitter hit me too hard," but will later retract the statement when pressed by the parents. Again, the child is probably afraid, of what the care giver will do to him and possibly of the parents' response as well.

HOW TO TELL IF YOUR CHILD'S BEEN A VICTIM OF PHYSICAL ABUSE

Besides the most obvious signs of physical abuse such as bruises and burns, there are other indications such as the following.

- *In infancy,* look for irritability and changes in behavior. If your baby was always easygoing and suddenly becomes clingy, crying and fussing for no apparent reason, it may be a sign of abuse.

- *In toddlers,* look for a change in behavior, particularly an unexplainable increase in aggressiveness and roughhousing. It's unusual and should be investigated, if parents don't use physical force and their mild-mannered child starts hitting and biting.

- *In school-age children,* again look for unexplained changes in behavior. Abused school-age children often show great anxiety and fear, they may have sleep problems and nightmares, and they may withdraw from play with their peers.

- *Adolescents and preadolescents* who are abused are often angry, expressing their feelings by acting-out and running away. They may also become severely depressed, and the depression can even culminate in suicidal acts.

An older child may have any number of reasons for not telling you about abuse; he may feel ashamed, afraid of your response, or afraid of the person who is abusing him. So even with an older child, don't count on getting all the facts directly.

WHAT TO DO IF YOU SEE SIGNS OF ABUSE

If you see any of these indications of possible abuse you should

- First take your child to your pediatrician. Explain the entire situation very carefully, and listen to his or her evaluation.

- Next take your child to a psychiatrist, counselor, or other mental-health worker for therapy and evaluation. Your child may be more communicative with a professional trained to evaluate and treat children with problems.

- If you believe your child is in an abusive situation, remove him from the situation without a moment's delay.

- At the very least, fire the care giver who is responsible. If the signs are blatant, you may even want to press charges.

SEXUAL ABUSE

A child who's been abused sexually will show all the above-mentioned symptoms of physical abuse. In addition, he or she may start playing with himself or herself in new ways—by obsessively masturbating, by inserting a finger in the rectum, etc.

Look for a higher incidence of anxiety in children between the ages of two and six, a level of anxiety that can even reach a state of panic. Small children who've been abused sexually may become almost paralyzed with fear; they may suffer severe stomachaches, headaches, and other psychosomatic symptoms; they may be afraid to leave the house. Older children and teenagers may, in addition, become extremely promiscuous in their own sexual behavior.

NEGLECT

Neglect is a much more subtle problem. A caretaker who is neglectful may simply watch television all day. Neglect is often very difficult to detect, particularly if it's been going on since birth or early infancy. Whereas a child who's been abused will have a reactive response, a neglected child will have a passive response.

Where a healthy six-month-old will smile at the approach of an adult, one who is neglected won't respond. He won't reach for things, he won't initiate activities. A child who is neglected may avoid eye contact. Early and continued neglect damages a child's ability to grow into a healthy, social human being.

And as a neglected child gets older, he will fail to achieve normal developmental milestones as well: His speech will be slow, he will be late in learning to crawl and walk and in developing fine motor skills, and as he reaches school age, he will have problems reading and learning.

If your child is displaying these symptoms of neglect, consult your pediatrician. He or she may recommend testing; sometimes physical problems can delay development. If there are no physical problems, you may well have a neglected child.

WHO IS A POTENTIAL ABUSER?

The terrifying answer is anyone. A child abuser may be an apparently sweet, grandmotherly woman, a teenage cousin, a friend of the family, or a certified daycare teacher. Yes, it could be anyone, but studies show that in most cases someone who is a child abuser was himself abused as a child.

When hiring a care giver, it may be impossible to elicit the background information necessary to know for certain that she will not abuse your child. But there are ways of making connections and listening between the lines. If you've hired someone, while you are training her or otherwise interacting, keep your eyes open, look and listen for her responses and any information she may tell you about her background. It's only prudent.

TWO CASES OF ABUSE

A three-and-a-half-year-old boy was referred to Dr. Jack Snyder because of a sudden onset of behavior problems. He was passive at home but he was hitting other children at the playground. There were no physical signs of abuse, but the parents were concerned even though the caretaker had been in their home for most of the child's life. According to Dr. Snyder, the parents suspected the childcare person was using overly punitive means of discipline on their child.

After a few sessions of play with the psychiatrist, the child was able to show him what was happening at home. The childcare person was immediately fired.

In another case, a two-and-a-half-year-old was referred to Dr. Snyder by a pediatrician because the child was having nightmares and exhibiting extremely fearful behavior. The parents were concerned because their child cowered in the crib even when they went near him.

The psychiatrist worked with the child and interviewed the au pair. She admitted to him that sometimes when the parents were away in the evening that she would drink and slap the child. When they were apprised of the truth of the situation, the family opted to retain the au pair, provided that she stop drinking and get help.

You, the parents, must decide the proper course of action when your child is abused by a care giver. Many people feel that one time is too many, that there are some actions that preclude forgiveness or a second chance. They feel that a child's safety and well-being come above all other considerations, and that one can never be certain that a care giver who has abused a child even one time will never do it again. Of course, there are other people, such as the above family who sought help for their care giver, who forgive, setting new conditions but continuing to employ the abusive care giver.

HOW TO FIRE A CARE GIVER

If there's one rule to follow about firing someone, it's to act decisively. Once you've made a decision that the person should go, don't hesitate; it will only prolong an unpleasant experience.

In many business situations, when a person is dismissed, the employer makes sure that the person leaves immediately. This is to ensure that the employee does not act out his or her frustrations or anger, particularly by destroying or stealing property.

How much more valuable is your child's well-being than office supplies, a computer, or a trade secret? Most parents would say that, while property has a price, a child is priceless. So why take chances that a resentful employee might—even if it's the remotest of possibilities—take any of her anger out on your child?

Often, parents who fire care givers and allow them to keep working for a week or two find that the worker's response is destructive. One single mother, who fired someone because the kids didn't like her, gave the care giver two weeks' notice. She thought it would both give her time to find someone new, and allow her to continue working at her own job. But it soon became clear that the care giver's resentment was like a powder keg, ready to explode. Faced with the dismissed worker's anger, she was forced to readjust her plans, finally paying the care giver two weeks' severance and staying home herself with the kids. It wasn't until the person was gone—really gone—that everyone in the family felt relieved.

Most people, short of a serious infraction (endangering the child, stealing, abuse, etc.) feel it's their responsibility to give a dismissed childcare worker notice in the form of a week's or two weeks' pay, along with accrued vacation time and severance (particularly if the person has been there for a long time and the employer just feels it's time to make a change). In situations where the parents are virtually certain that there will be no hard feelings, people often keep the care giver on for up to a month, both to allow her time to find a new job and to find a replacement themselves.

Many parents, when there is not an emergency situation, prepare for a dismissal by interviewing for a replacement in advance, arranging to be home themselves, or making temporary alternate childcare plans. They are then able to say goodbye immediately, without being dependent on the dismissed care giver a moment longer than is absolutely necessary.

WHAT ABOUT THE CHILDREN?

What do you say to your child when you fire a childcare person? It depends on the situation in your home, the circumstances that led to the dismissal, the age of your child, the level of involvement and attachment your child feels toward the care giver, and other, more subtle, personality factors.

If you fired a person in large part because your older children didn't like her, of course you would expect to discuss the situation with them to whatever extent you deem appropriate. If, however, you fired her for other reasons not directly related to your children's feelings, it's your responsibility, even if you feel awkward about it, to communicate why the childcare person is gone (your kids are going to find out anyway, so it's best to be direct). But don't expect that telling them is going to close the book; even at the age of eleven, twelve, or thirteen your children are still likely to have separation problems—much like in a divorce.

If you fired a baby sitter for an infant who was showing no signs of attachment, then it's probably unnecessary to say anything at all, other than "So and so won't be coming anymore," and being there to introduce and orient the baby to the new care giver.

But once a child is attached it's not always so simple. Even in preverbal children, there is a feeling of loss that parents should be sensitive to. And telling a child (ranging in age from a toddler to school age) that someone who has been taking care of him is going to leave, is difficult even if the leave-taking is a positive one; in the case of a firing it's a very sensitive subject.

"I wouldn't necessarily tell the child the person was fired," says child psychiatrist Dr. William Koch. "Separation is what the child is feeling. He may be angry at mom because the person is gone and feeling guilty that he caused her to go away. And if you let the child know that the person was fired the message is, 'If you sent her away, you can send me away.' Make it clear to your child that this can never be; that mommy loves you and will always be with you, even if other people go away."

Elaine Ruskin of New York's West Side Y says that if a person was caught stealing or was fired for specific cause, "The reason she left is secondary. All the child knows is that he was abandoned." She suggests that you allow your child to feel and express his feelings, to draw him out, by saying, for example, "Mommy is sad; I know you're sad."

Fretta Reitzes of the 92nd Street Y Parenting Center adds, "You have to communicate to your kids that you're their anchor and that other people come to help them."

In short, when you fire someone, all you should tell a small child is that the childcare person isn't going to be here anymore. The reasons "why" are adult issues and should remain that way.

Your child may be hurt, or feel abandoned, or be angry; he may not like the fact that the childcare person is gone. It's important that you let him know it's okay to feel his feelings, no matter what they are. Ask your child how he feels. He may not respond. If necessary, you can lead him to the point where he is comfortable enough to express his feelings. Say it's okay to feel bad, it's okay to be angry. By giving your child the room to feel and express his emotions, you will also be giving him the opportunity to quickly regain the sense of being secure and loved by the people who will always be there, his parents.

CHAPTER 9

Saying Goodbye

When you love someone, leaving hurts, no matter how old you are. A toddler feels the loss of someone he loves—even if he can't yet talk about it. A teenager, faced with the inevitable departure of the nurturing woman she's known since babyhood, mourns. A mother, betrayed by a person she thought of as a friend, puts on a protective coat of emotional armor and chalks up another loss to experience.

People cope with loss in different ways. Sometimes they allow themselves pain, feel grief, and grow stronger emotionally. Sometimes they withdraw emotionally rather than allowing themselves to experience strong feelings; often they become angry to avoid feeling abandonment.

When a favorite baby sitter leaves, it affects entire families, not just children. But children don't have the experience adults have, and they frequently need the guidance of sympathetic grown-ups to feel their feelings, learn from the experience, and keep going. As parents, we should have the internal resources to cope with the loss of our children's care giver, as well as enough sensitivity to give comfort, allow feelings to be felt and help our kids to move on.

EASING THE PAIN OF PARTING

As a parent, it's sometimes necessary to call on your own reserves of sensitivity and intuition to comfort your child and help him through a separation. There is no formula for helping children live with loss—would that it were that easy.

Even child development professionals disagree on specific ways you can prepare your children for separation and help them through the painful period of mourning. (And it is true mourning, for although the object of grief remains alive, she's somewhere else; she's no longer part of the child's life.)

The first fact, which is agreed on by everyone we spoke with, is that whether a childcare person is fired, leaves of her own free will, or because of a decision you made about your needs, separation is what the child will experience. Even if a person was abusive or negligent, the child's feelings of relief will be tempered by a feeling of loss.

"Kids are most anxious about being abandoned," says developmental psychologist Dr. Irving Sigel. "Not only children . . . adults too are unprepared for loss. Even if you have a friend who's dying of cancer, you're never fully prepared for the end."

Never fully prepared, but capable of coping. When your children love someone and she leaves, they feel pain—abandonment, separation, and anxiety. But there are things parents can do to help, and children do have the resiliency—as long as they have the support of a loving family—to not feel shattered. As Dr. William Koch explains, "A child has an ego by the age of three and can deal with separation and loss." That's good news for parents.

PREPARING FOR THE INEVITABLE

Dr. Irving Sigel cautions, "Don't talk about separation in advance. Don't say 'your childcare person will leave someday'; it will only create anxiety. But do tell your child about your care giver's family. If she has children encourage her to bring them over. Let your child know that his care giver has a life outside your family."

Other experts believe that if your child brings up the subject of the care giver leaving, that it should be addressed directly. Child psychiatrist Dr. Gail Wasserman goes even further, suggesting that parents initiate the discussion. "If a child is over two," she says, "she should know that the person will leave at some point. As soon as the child is ready, she should be told that the childcare person is not the child's mother—she's the housekeeper—and someday she may do other things. It is hoped then if the person leaves it will not come as such a great shock to the child. But the mother, on the other hand, should not be shocked if the child is upset."

What it all boils down to is this: You prepare your child for separation in the most sensitive way you can. If you feel it's best to talk about the inevitable from the first, fine, but do so in a way that's responsive to your child's feelings. Children need a sense of security; if you give them a message of impermanence you're certainly not helping, and you may be damaging their ability to form attachments.

If your intuition tells you to wait until an explanation is necessary, then it probably is the best road for you and your child. Guidelines are subjective; psychology is an imprecise science. Everyone can, and does, disagree. But the absence of precise guidelines is not a license to abdicate your responsibility to your child. Look inside yourself: If your decisions are based simply on what makes you comfortable, what's easiest for you, then you are being irresponsible; look instead beyond yourself to what will make your child feel best.

A PERIOD OF TRANSITION

From the time you learn (or decide) that your care giver is going to leave, until your child has settled into a new routine—whether at school, with a different baby sitter, with mom at home, or in a new city—there are numerous ways you can lend support and show your love for your child.

Psychologist Frances Bick suggests that you tell your child the reason (if it can be understood and accepted) before the baby sitter leaves. Dr. William Koch believes an older child deserves (and will demand) an explanation, but all you have to tell a younger child is that the childcare person is not going to be here anymore, and that "all the reasons are adult issues." Dr. Irving Sigel says, "If a child-care person leaves, just say we're all going to miss her."

Whatever you decide to tell your child about the reasons for his care giver's departure, it's essential for you to be consistent. Don't say one thing one day, only to contradict yourself the next. Your child needs your consistency in explaining things, but even more important is your constancy, your availability, to reassure him that you will always be there. Make it clear that he can always count on his family, that even if others come and go you will never leave.

Even if you are the most consistent and loving parents in the world, you're not going to be able to protect your child from difficult painful feelings. Trying to prevent these feelings from surfacing make them go away, it will just drive them underground. And us that are buried inevitably come up again, often in dis-d destructive forms. No matter how difficult it is for you to r child to express feelings of loss, it's essential. Let your cry, and scream—and be there to help work those hard-elings out.

d loves someone, and particularly if the love is recipro-hat person may bring about a time of nightmares, unexplained crying, or lashing out with anger. The feelings of abandonment that cause those inexplicable actions are real. And the problems are not just limited to small children; even a child of twelve or thirteen will have separation problems, much like in the aftermath of a divorce.

But with you there, eventually the anger will fade and the pain will pass. As Heather, an English nanny, said, "I make sure I work for parents who are involved with their kids. It's easy to leave the job if you know a child will be happy."

Margaret, a young West Indian care giver, recognizes the enormity of the tasks facing the two-and-a-half-year-old boy she cares for whose family is moving to another city. "Of course I'm concerned," she says. "I'm very attached to Danny, just as he is to me. He's got a lot to deal with now—he's leaving his home, his friends, his baby sitter. We have a few months to prepare, and I just want to be able to help him through his move."

KEEPING IN TOUCH AFTER THE CARE GIVER LEAVES

What should you do after the fact? Dr. William Koch says, "You can start by asking the child how he feels. He may be angry at you because the childcare person is gone and feeling guilty that he caused her to go away. He may not say anything. You can say, 'Lots of boys and girls would be angry that [their baby sitter] left. . . . It's okay to be angry."

Many parents and childcare experts agree with Dr. Koch that it's the parents' responsibility to draw their children out, helping them to articulate their feelings so that they can come to terms with them. However, Dr. Gail Wasserman disagrees.

She suggests that you "wait for the signals from your child. The child may not regress or feel distressed. If the child is okay, leave him alone, don't bring up his feelings about the person who left."

"Words may not be the best way to deal with it," she says. "Maybe you just have to spend more time with your child for a while."

Eventually, even if a child doesn't talk about them at first, feelings do come to the surface. Just because it takes a child time to articulate feelings, it doesn't mean they aren't there.

Jill, the mother of a four-year-old boy, spoke about the effects of their family's move from New York to Los Angeles. "We were surprised . . . when we left he was okay about it at the time; it was later that he really felt the loss and wanted her back."

Most parents (and many baby sitters, if they've left on good terms) try to ease the pain of parting by doing something concrete. The parents arrange for goodbye parties, help their child choose a goodbye gift, or take pictures of the childcare person so that they may be shown to the child when he needs to be reminded of his former baby sitter. The care giver leaves a token of herself to remember her by; in addition she visits, calls, or writes to help ease the adjustment. If there's one thing virtually all the child development experts agreed on, it's that these concrete actions help.

EXPERIENCES AND REMINISCENCES

When baby sitter Betty told Sarah's mother that she was getting married and would soon leave, Sarah, not yet a year and a half old, was just starting to talk. She had a very strong personality (her mother called her "headstrong"). She knew what she wanted, and did everything she could to get it. She was the type of child who would both run over and hold onto mommy when she needed reinforcement and turn her plate upside down if she didn't like what she was fed for dinner. And Betty, whom the mother described as "dependable and loving, but into control," always wanted her to have lunch at the same time every day. Despite their seemingly antithetical personalities, Sarah was very attached to Betty.

Although Sarah was not yet truly verbal, her parents, who were extremely sensitive to their child's emotional needs, explained to her as well as they could that Betty would be leaving, that she was getting married and moving away. "No," said Sarah. She wouldn't permit it.

"My Betty, my Betty," she cried when the baby sitter next arrived at work, and she clung to Betty all day.

The parents took pictures of Betty and showed them to Sarah. Betty gave Sarah presents to remember her by. And when she left, she kept in touch, calling on the phone and visiting occasionally.

Sarah adapted much more quickly than her parents thought she would. Although she withdrew temporarily and lost some of her aggressiveness, she was very resilient. She was happy to hear from Betty, but she soon became attached to her new, more-flexible and easygoing, baby sitter. And by the time she was two, all she remembered of Betty were the pictures.

Kelly is a self-assured, social, happy child with a winning smile and a need to know why that's natural for an uninhibited three-year-old. From the time he was a baby, he was taken care of in his parents' absence by Iris, a West Indian woman his mother's age.

Iris was warm and perceptive; she was a professional care giver, who had previously worked in the home of one family for many years, until their youngest child went to school. And Kelly's mother always assumed that Iris would stay with them for many years as well.

Thus it came as a shock when Iris announced to Kelly's parents that she intended to leave. She had been working as a baby sitter for ten years, she explained, and she now felt it was time to move on. She wanted more time with her own children and she also wanted to train for a more prestigious career. She planned to go to school and take a job closer to home, but first she was planning to go home and visit her parents for a month. Her last day would be in ten weeks.

The parents' first response was anger. They felt hurt and abandoned. Hadn't they always accommodated her needs? Hadn't they given her time off when she needed it to deal with her immigration status, hadn't they made temporary arrangements (and paid her for far more than the standard number of sick days), when she was disabled for a month with an injury? How could she do this to them? If they could find a replacement right away, they would just as soon cut it off—and cut their losses—immediately.

Within days, their mood had tempered. Iris had been great for Kelly for three years. She had given them plenty of notice, and had real reasons for wanting to leave. They decided to try to accommodate her needs.

They offered her a large raise, bringing her salary above that of any other job she could get. Since Kelly was about to start a half-day preschool program, they also offered to adjust her hours to allow her to attend college in the mornings. They offered various other inducements, but Iris had her mind made up; she wouldn't budge.

Three weeks before she was scheduled to leave, Kelly's parents told him that Iris would be leaving. When he asked why she was going, they patiently went over the reasons: She wanted to see her mommy and daddy who lived in Jamaica, she needed to be closer to her children (whom Kelly idolized), and she was going to study to be a nurse. They also told him that Iris loved him, but that she felt she had to do these things for herself and her own family. And that even though Iris was leaving, mommy and daddy would never leave, but would always be there for him whenever he needed them.

He broke into tears, and when he finally stopped crying he said he didn't want Iris to go. Then he asked again—why? But the next day, when his parents asked him how he felt, he said he was all right.

Once, a few days later, Kelly told his parents he was angry at Iris for leaving, but other than that he avoided the subject, saying either that he didn't want to talk about it or that he was fine. For a short period he woke up at night and had trouble going back to sleep. One night he told his mother a dream: The walls of the house were falling down around him. But it wasn't a really bad dream, he said.

Kelly's mother decided to give Iris a going-away party. Kelly picked out a "good luck" cake, the mother bought her a present, and a few of Kelly's friends, whose care givers were friendly with his baby sitter, came over to say goodbye.

Lots of pictures were taken (the parents wanted to keep them for Kelly to remember Iris by), the children played, the adults talked, and for over an hour the soon-to-be-ex-baby sitter walked around with misty eyes. Finally, after everyone else had left and she was saying goodbye to the family, she broke into tears and held Kelly close, with love. They walked her down to the subway, three adults and a child all crying.

The next morning Kelly's father called Iris and asked her once again if she would think about reconsidering. But she had made up her mind, and they didn't hold out much hope.

When asked how he felt in the next days and weeks, Kelly always said he was fine. And when his parents finally got around to interviewing for a care giver, he patiently explained to each applicant that he needed a new baby sitter, and was unfailingly polite and friendly with each of them.

But occasionally, he would just start crying for no apparent reason. He didn't like to talk about it, he had a strong family center, his parents were careful to not threaten his sense of security, and he himself obviously wanted to move on. But the hurt of the loss lingered.

More than a year later, after a new care giver (and a new baby) had become part of Kelly's life, he still looked forward to the occasions when Iris and her children visited. She was no longer someone he needed everyday, but had become a favorite friend—like an aunt—who continued to love him dearly and whom he continued to love in return.

Philip was angry. He felt abandoned by Lena, the one person who had always been there, providing a calm center while his family's emotional storm raged about him. His parents were often distracted, racing about trying to make ends meet, but somehow Lena never seemed to get flustered even when everyone else around was losing their heads. And so he felt betrayed when his parents took her away, virtually handing her over to a neighborhood family with a baby.

They really had no choice. With two kids in private school (Philip was seven, his sister Grace fourteen), they didn't have the money to spare. And they felt that with Philip in school all day (and with the availability of after-school care on school premises), he really didn't need someone to be at home anymore anyway.

Philip had been taken care of by Lena since he was a baby. She had given him guidance, responded to his quick, funny, nervous ways with appreciation and sympathy, and in short, loved him. She had a child of her own, a daughter exactly his age. He and Lena's daughter had become friendly, playing together frequently when Lena's own childcare arrangements broke down. So he knew Lena had her own family, but it never bothered him; she still felt permanent to him. She was his ally, and he couldn't understand why she would ever want to leave.

In actuality she didn't. Philip's mother had urged Lena to find something new for herself over a year earlier, but she had stayed on, sharing her time between his family and another family in the building for most of that year. She almost had to be pushed to leave. So Philip had lots of warning that Lena would eventually move on.

The parting was long and protracted, with plenty of notice. And although everyone was sensitive to Philip's feelings, he was angry anyway. He was sullen at times, aggressive at other times; he gained weight and occasionally acted as though he had lost his moorings.

His sister, on the other hand, couldn't care less; she had always felt that Lena was Philip's baby sitter, and besides, she was growing into a fiercely independent teenager.

After Lena left the job, she still came to visit on occasion, and sometimes she and the baby she was now responsible for would pick Philip up at school in the afternoon and take him to the playground. But it wasn't the same. After clinging to her the first few times they saw each other (after she left his family), he began to put some distance between them. Lena was no longer a constant in his life, no longer someone he could count on, and he began to make the adjustments necessary to survive the rest of his life without her.

Agnes was as much a part of the family as a baby sitter could be. Although she came from a different cultural background from Jennifer's, she was always there, a constant source of love and support.

Agnes was from an old New England family that had fallen on hard times during the Great Depression. She had come to New York many years earlier, and when her husband died, leaving her child-less, she decided to stay and make her own way in the world. She took a job with a young first-generation family, immigrant's children who were working their way into the professional middle class.

She was hired soon after Charley and Helen's first child was born. And she stayed, and watched as the child grew. A few years later, the little girl had a brother, and five years after that came the baby, Jennifer.

Agnes was a constant presence in the household, always there to make sure that the children dressed properly, that they ate well, that they did their homework, and that they were polite to their elders and considerate of other children. The parents said how they never worried when their kids were with Agnes, that they knew she would take care of them with common sense and love. Agnes became indispensable, a member of the family.

And the first child grew up, and when she left to go to college, leaving Agnes was part of her passage into adulthood. And when her younger brother was ready to follow her to college, everyone, Agnes as well as the parents, felt that the baby sitter had done her job. She had been working for one family for over twenty years, and she and they agreed, now it was time for her to go home. Everyone agreed, that is, except for the baby of the family, now thirteen.

Jennifer wasn't grown up; she was just passing into adolescence, and she felt cheated. Agnes was there until her sister left, she reasoned, she was there till her brother left. Somehow she always assumed that Agnes would be there for her too until she was ready to leave. She was devastated. (Not that the leave-taking was easy for Agnes, or for the parents either, for that matter. They had all grown to know each other's ways so well. The relationship had been part of the landscape of their lives for so long, and seeing it end was painful for all of them.) For Jennifer, though, it was as if a parent were suddenly exiled, or had abandoned the family.

But they kept in touch. Jennifer and Agnes spoke on the telephone frequently, and Jennifer spoke about how she could feel the older woman listening to, and sympathizing with, the changes taking place in her life. She even visited twice the first year, taking a bus by herself to the small Maine town where Agnes was born and had retired. Agnes visited too; she was homesick herself for the family that had been her family for over two decades.

But gradually the bonds loosened, the phone calls became less frequent, the visits (there was only one trip to Maine the second year) ceased, and Agnes became like a distant, fondly remembered relative, not a part of everyday life.

And by the time Jennifer was fifteen, her life was filled with her friends, and her family, and her future. But the future had a past that she would never forget.

Jennifer and her parents spoke about the parting two years after the fact. It was still fresh in their minds, and Jennifer herself spoke with an openness that made clear both the wounds of the separation (now healing) and the wonderful sense that she had had something special in her life that she would always treasure.

A father reminisces about his own experience of separation. "I'll never forget when we moved. I was six, my sister was eight. Our parents had been divorced no more than a few months, and I missed my father. Now we were being uprooted to be closer to my mother's family. But my family was staying behind.

"Ethel Mae had taken care of us for two and a half years. She was a big, loud, southern black woman with a big heart and a real knack for making a child feel safe. I remember all the times she threatened to hit us with a switch if we didn't mind—she never did and I'm sure she never seriously considered it—but just the idea that she cared enough about our well-being to chase us down the street waving that thing made us feel better. Everytime.

"She helped my mother pack the car, and then gave us both big hugs and kisses to remember her by. We were all crying. And then—and I'll remember this as long as I live—we got into the car and started to drive away. I looked out the window—I was crying so hard I could barely see—and Ethel Mae was there, just standing there, watching us. And the tears were streaming down her cheeks as we drove away.

"My father came back into my life periodically. He's been dead for a long time now . . . and I do miss him. Ethel Mae . . . I don't recall ever speaking to her again. But I've mourned her loss all my life. I still miss her."

PARTING IS SUCH SWEET SORROW

Separation from a loved one resonates well beyond the actual time of the separation. The person whose existence once brought a child joy, but whose loss caused anger, or pain, or sadness, can be remembered with love long past childhood's end, or she can be quickly relegated to the deepest recesses of memory, where trauma is buried. If the relationship was a strong one, and the parting served to reinforce the positive nature of the experience, then the memory will linger, and the lessons learned by loving will remain inside the heart.

Parting is not just an end, it's a new beginning too. It's a demarcation point, a time when a child passes from one phase of his life to another.

If a child's experience with a care giver was the kind we all wish for our children, then the love will remain, and the special relationship that existed between a child and an adult will enrich the child's life, and be remembered with love, forever. The best you can hope for from your children's experience with in-home childcare is that they will remember how another person touched their lives, giving them love and getting love from them in return. Then this central experience of their formative years will be one that they can hold onto as a treasure for the rest of their lives.

CHAPTER 10

The Business of Childcare

When you hire an in-home childcare worker, you become an employer. As such, you are required to follow the laws of the land concerning taxation, immigration, fair wages, and other employment practices.

But as we all know, the law of the land is often ignored, even in the highest places. What should be and what actually exists are often two entirely different things. And most parents, whether they themselves participate in it or not, are aware of the large gray market in household employment, through which many people (both employers and employees) avoid taxes and ignore immigration regulations. Although we do not sanction such practices, we can't deny the fact that they exist.

IMMIGRATION ISSUES

Historically, an extremely large percentage of childcare workers have been undocumented immigrants. This is true all over the country. In the Southwest, for example, vast numbers of undocumented workers from Mexico and Central America work in other people's homes. In the Northeast, the same is true of workers from the West Indies.

Many people, particularly those from poor countries, just want to live in the United States. They are willing to accept poor wages and working conditions simply for the privilege of being here. This fact, as well as the economic benefits enjoyed by their employers, accounts for the large numbers of people working in this country without legal immigration papers.

The first fact of life for illegal immigrants is that they have to hide, that they have to be, in effect, "nonpersons." In order to hide their presence more effectively, as well as because it is often the only job they can get, many undocumented immigrants live as well as work in the homes of their employers. They are paid in cash; they are not responsible for rent, telephone, electricity, and other bills that people with their own households have to pay; they are virtually invisible.

This situation, of frightened workers unprotected by the umbrella of American social services that benefits other workers, is one that can easily be taken advantage of by employers. Of course, some people pay fair market wages and provide good working and living conditions to illegal immigrants. But, because the situation provides the temporary benefit of United States residence for workers who would otherwise be unable to stay in the country, it's a way many employers pay low wages while demanding high productivity. Desperation is an open invitation to exploitation.

EFFECTS OF THE 1986 IMMIGRATION LAW

This was true before the passage of the new immigration law, and it's still true. But that's not to say there is no change in the (unwritten) rules of the game; there are significant changes taking place right now concerning the status of immigrant labor.

Perhaps most important, the Immigration Reform and Control Act of 1986 provided amnesty and legal status for those previously undocumented workers who lived in the United States continuously from before January 1, 1982 through the amnesty registration period. This provision didn't affect every immigrant, by any means, but it has begun to have a far-reaching effect on household employment throughout the country. It is estimated that 3.9 million people were eligible for immigration amnesty. The *New York Times* reported that, in July 1987 alone, over 40,000 undocumented U.S. residents a week applied to become permanent, legal residents.

Obviously, not all illegal aliens work as care givers, but clearly a lot of them do. And with the sheer numbers of workers who applied for legal status—a number in the hundreds of thousands—it was inevitable that many people who were previously employed illegally as in-home childcare workers changed their status.

With the passage and implementation of the 1986 immigration law, part of the underground economy in household help moved aboveground, as numerous workers applied for immigration amnesty. Amnesty and legal status mean a person has access to protection under Social Security, unemployment, and other federal employment programs, as well as Medicaid, food stamps, and other social services previously denied by her "nonpersonhood." It's no wonder, then, that long-time live-in care givers were among those who took advantage of the amnesty program.

For parents who previously employed live-in off-the-books workers (often at a fraction of the legal minimum wage), this came as an awful shock. For even though the employers may have wished to continue with the same arrangement as before, their household workers, freed from the necessity of working sixty to seventy hours a week for $100, began to look elsewhere for work.

For those who have always complied with the law (paying legal workers legal wages for legal work hours, filing tax forms with state and federal authorities and paying taxes), the change in the immigration law has had little direct effect, other than perhaps increasing the supply of legally qualified workers.

Immediately after the amnesty period, our conviction that many workers, once given the choice, would choose to take advantage of the laws protecting them was confirmed in reality. One New York household employment agency, which began checking green cards (as the law requires), reported having a host of new live-out job applicants, most of whom chose to leave live-in situations as soon as their status became legal.

IMMIGRATION COMPLIANCE

You may still hire an illegal alien and pay her off-the-books. But it's more difficult than before. You, as an employer, are now legally required to do more. According to the Immigration and Naturalization Service's (INS) *Handbook for Employers*, "The law says that you should hire only American citizens and aliens who are authorized to work in the United States." One of the changes written into the new law is that you, the employer, need to verify the employment eligibility of anyone hired after November 6, 1986.

In practice, this means that both you and your employee are required to fill out the INS Employment Eligibility Verification Form I-9. You must check documents that establish identity and employment eligibility for any worker you hire after the above date. Employers who violate the law may face civil or criminal penalties.

LABOR CERTIFICATION

In order for an alien not eligible for the amnesty provisions of the Immigration Reform and Control Act of 1986 to receive an immigration visa (also known as lawful permanent residence or a "green card"—now actually pink), he or she must prove that (1) there are not sufficient U.S. workers who are able, willing, qualified, and available for the employment, and (2) his or her employment will not adversely effect the wages and working conditions of U.S. workers similarly employed.

Workers who meet these qualifications are issued individual (job offer) labor certifications; those who do not are placed in the "Schedule B" category (occupations in general oversupply). Throughout the United States, U.S. labor certifications for Schedule B applicants are generally denied.

Childcare workers fall under the umbrella classification of "Household Domestic Service Workers"; in general, household workers are classified under Schedule B. If, however, a person has "one year of documented full-time paid experience in the task to be performed," she then becomes eligible for an individual labor certification. The one-year requirement is intended to ensure that the worker knows the demands unique to household employment and is likely to continue working in the field after becoming certified. In addition, there is one very serious proviso: In order for certification to be viable in terms of a lack of U.S. workers available for the job, the position must be live-in. Live-out household domestic service workers are rarely approved for certification. The Labor Department and the INS, however, rarely investigate whether a household worker really lives-in.

The catch-22 in this law is self-evident; many workers who are being sponsored are not legally living or working in the United States, because they came to this country under a visitor's or other short-term visa. Because they need to have a year "of documented full-time paid experience" in their field before applying for certification, they need to either get the experience illegally, or be able to document their work in the field outside the United States.

Some parents help their childcare workers obtain legal status. If you want to do so, it's good to be aware that it's a relatively arduous process, in which the requirements of not only the Labor Department and the INS, but possibly also the State Department and American consulates overseas, must be satisfied. Because of the legal complexities involved, we suggest that an employer not try to muddle through the morass alone. If you really want to obtain labor certification (and legal status) for your care giver, you should take your case to an immigration lawyer.

AU PAIRS—THE EXCEPTION

Because foreign au pairs are not applying for permanent resident status in the United States, they do not fall under the same classification as immigrants who wish to stay here indefinitely. Some au pairs come in on student (F-1) visas. The conditions of this visa include the stipulation that the student must have financial backing. As such, these students are not legally permitted to work in this country.

Au pairs who are enrolled in the legal au pair programs (see appendix B) enter the United States with J-1 cultural exchange visas, which are good for twelve months. They must return to their native country when their visas expire. Other au pairs enter the country on tourist visas and then remain to become part of the undocumented immigrant work force.

PAYING YOUR CARE GIVER

Wage scales for childcare workers are far from uniform. They vary from city to city, even from neighborhood to neighborhood within the same city; they depend on job description and category (nanny, au pair), on status (on-the-books/off-the-books, live-in/live-out), on experience, ages of children, length of time employed, hours worked, and special duties performed. Therefore, there's no standard wage for care givers, as with, for example, production-line workers. And it's impossible for us to say, "This is what you have to pay your care giver." But here are some general observations about pay scales.

- The federal legal minimum wage (as of 1989) was $3.35 an hour. Household workers, although not covered by federal minimum wage laws, are included within the minimum wage guidelines of many states.

- In the case of in-home childcare, the Labor Department stipulates that you can deduct up to $15 a week for room and $21 a week for food from the total salary. According to the Labor Department, the prevailing wage for live-in help is $5.47 an hour for a 44-hour week.

- If you're hiring an experienced live-out care giver in a major city, you can expect to pay more than double the minimum wage.

- People in larger cities tend to pay more than those in smaller cities.

- Pay scales are higher in affluent neighborhoods than in less-affluent communities.

- People with more children (particularly twins) or disabled children, families whose homes are not convenient to public transportation, and people with large homes and extended housekeeping duties all can expect to pay a premium for skilled, experienced workers.

- Trained nannies are the highest paid in-home childcare workers, followed by professional childcare worker/housekeepers. In upper-middle-class, big city or suburban neighborhoods (in metropolitan regions such as New York, Washington, D.C., and Boston), nannies often receive well over

$300 per week (plus benefits) and occasionally as much as $400 to $500; experienced live-out care givers have begun to approach the same over $300 wage level for a forty- to fifty-hour workweek. Au pairs, on the other hand, may get little more than room, board, and transportation but salaries may range from $100 to $200 per week.

WHAT SHOULD YOU PAY?

That's a good question and one we can't answer. Clearly, to a large extent it depends on the experience and qualifications of the particular person you're employing, as well as on the specific demands of the job. It also depends on where you live.

It's generally not very hard to find out the norms for your community: Ask your friends what they pay their care givers; take your child to the neighborhood playground (or go there yourself) and speak with other parents; call an agency that provides your area with childcare workers. A little investigation may tell you a lot. (And if you still don't know, you can bet your care giver probably does.)

RAISES

Most people give their care givers a raise at the end of the trial period. Often the salary increase is as little as $10 per week (although it's sometimes as much as $25 or more), but even if it's only a token, it makes a significant statement: You are saying to her that she is permanent, that she is valued, and that she can expect to be rewarded for taking good care of your children and your home.

After the initial raise, most employers give their childcare workers annual increases. These range from basic cost of living adjustments to significant raises based on your care giver's increasing importance in your household. If you want to keep your baby sitter happy (or even keep your baby sitter), you should also expect to give some kind of compensation every time you increase her responsibilities. If you have a new baby, or want her to do more of the cleaning, or ask her to come in earlier or stay later, it's wise to give her some kind of raise. In addition, several employer/parents told us that their personal policy was, when the mother or father got an increase in salary, so did the care giver.

HOURS OF WORK

What are usual and fair expectations for the number of hours childcare workers should work? Many childcare employees work long hours, often from before the parents go to work in the morning until after they come home in the evening. It's not unusual for a care giver to have a standard 8:00 A.M. to 6:00 P.M., fifty-hour-a-week job. The hours you expect your childcare person to work should be made clear to her before she actually starts the job, and if at anytime you must make a significant change in her hours, it's something that is likely to bring about a basic renegotiation of her contract.

Many live-in (particularly undocumented) childcare workers put in hours that are even longer than the usual long care giver hours, often working from early in the morning until late at night. This is not, however, the usual practice; most employers recognize that the people who work for them need time for themselves and most baby sitters, faced with an unbearable work load, inevitably look for a more reasonable job. Seventy- or eighty-hour workweeks are not only unusual, they're also illegal in many states. (In California, for example, anything above nine hours in a workday requires time and a half for overtime, as does the sixth workday in a week.)

Permanent part-time childcare workers generally have set hours of work, for example, five afternoons a week from 12:00 P.M. to

5:30 P.M. This arrangement enables parents to pay people only for the time they are actually needed. (In the above example, it allows the parent of a preschooler in a morning program to take her child to school in the morning and have someone to pick him up and take care of him in the afternoon.)

Part-time care givers are generally compensated in much the same way that full-time workers are, with a weekly salary based on an hourly figure. In addition to the salary, many parents include benefits, such as a paid vacation and holidays, for the care givers they rely on, even if they are only part-time.

For those employers who want their childcare people to work flexible hours, the situation is a little more complex. Having a person on call all the time is, in most cases, if not completely out of the question then at least the source of a huge amount of tension. And if you don't want to pay someone for time she doesn't actually work, you are leaving yourself open to the almost inevitable day when you need her desperately and she has other plans.

It's important to structure any childcare employment situation with flexible hours in such a way that you are covered when you really need to be, and she is satisfied that the arrangement will also take care of her needs. In order to accomplish both these goals, it makes sense to set both minimum and maximum number of work hours in advance; by making it part of the contract, she knows that you are responsible for giving her a certain number of hours (and dollars) each week. It's also wise to give her as much advance notice as possible as to the specific hours you expect her to work. (It is completely unfair to call her at nine and expect her to come in at ten.)

EXTRA PAY, GIFTS, AND BONUSES

Generally, if childcare workers stay late, or work extra days, they are paid extra money. Some parents follow the guidelines for other (nonhousehold) workers, paying time and a half for overtime and weekends. Others pay straight time. In situations where the person is an illegal immigrant working off-the-books, there is more of an incidence of people not paying extra for longer hours.

In many cities, asking an employee to stay later than usual can create significant transportation problems for her in getting home. In order to help ensure that the care giver will stay late when needed, employers often pay the extra transportation costs as well as overtime pay.

In our research for this book, we asked hundreds of parents whether they gave bonuses and gifts, and what they considered appropriate. The vast majority of those who responded gave either annual bonuses or occasional gifts to their care givers. Many gave both.

Gifts were given for birthdays, Christmas, and occasionally just to say "thank you." They included clothing, kitchen equipment, and toys for the care giver's own children.

Cash bonuses, generally given at Christmas time, ranged in our survey from $10 or $20 for short-term, part-time employees to much more substantial sums—one, two, or even three weeks' pay—for permanent, long-term care givers.

Why should you give your care giver gifts and a bonus? Most people like to feel appreciated and it's one of the best ways you can show your appreciation for the important job she's doing taking care of your children.

TIME OFF

Again, if you're not concerned with fairness, or with keeping a good employee satisfied, you can pay a care giver only for the actual days she works. But we don't advise it, either on ethical or on practical grounds. A person who is a regular employee merits time off with pay—a vacation, sick days, and holidays.

Most full-time care givers prefer having weekends or two other consecutive days off. Because the standard workweek for white-collar and professional jobs is a five-day week with Saturday and Sunday off, this preference usually coincides with the employer family's needs. And it certainly wouldn't make sense for you to give your childcare person her days off when you have to go in to work.

VACATION

Most parents give full-time workers at least one week's paid vacation for the first year; many give two weeks. If a person's been working for you for several years, you might increase the paid vacation to three weeks.

As a practical matter, it makes sense to require that your care giver's vacation coincide with your own, and many parents make that condition clear from the start of the care giver's employment. Some families who give two weeks' paid vacation stipulate that half of it must coincide with their own time off, while allowing the other week to be taken at the discretion of the care giver.

People who go away frequently, taking long weekends during the summer or bringing their families along on business trips, often pay their household employees for the time they're away. Indeed, those who don't are asking for trouble. And if your family is going away for an extended period (on a two-month summer vacation, for example) and you don't pay your care giver, you're likely to lose her.

Au pairs and mother's helpers generally join their employers on vacation. In fact, this is often considered to be one of the benefits of the job. But it should not be viewed as a vacation for the au pair.

For a part-time employee, a general rule of thumb might be to give her one day's paid vacation for each day of the week she works in your home. If you have a regular care giver, however, who works for you two or three full days a week or more, it's reasonable to follow the same guidelines as you would for a full-time employee, with her vacation computed according to her usual workweek.

PAID HOLIDAYS

Permanent care givers generally get the same holidays that the general labor force gets: New Year's, Memorial Day, the Fourth of July, Labor Day, Thanksgiving, Christmas, and a couple of other discretionary holidays such as Martin Luther King Day, President's Day, Good Friday, or the employee's birthday.

SICK DAYS

Many parent/employers don't specify the number of paid sick days they give their childcare employees. If a person is sick, they reason, she's sick. This system works in many instances, but it can be abused. On the other hand, your home does not function like a large corporation; rules can be flexible and relationships are personal. Even if your "contract" with your care giver specifies five paid sick days a year, you can use your discretion in expanding the time off with pay. For example, if your baby sitter has always taken minimal sick days and one year she has a bout of illness that keeps her out of work for an extended period, you may find it to be in your interest (as well as hers) to extend the sick benefits. And one family we spoke with uses a bonus system regarding sick days: Their care giver is paid for every allotted sick day *not* taken during the course of the year.

UNPAID LEAVE

There are numerous reasons why your childcare worker may want
to take an extended leave of absence. She may have immigration
problems that require her complete attention, she may be pregnant
or have a new baby, or she may have a family emergency.

You're not required to give someone a leave of absence, and in fact
there are a lot of reasons why you might not want to do it. Your
children are forced to make adjustments, both to the new temporary person you most likely will hire and to the old care giver once
she returns. You have someone in your house who doesn't know
your routine, whom you have to train, and who is likely to be gone
as soon as she gets the hang of the job. The general caliber and
trustworthiness of temporary care is usually lower than those who
want permanent jobs. And when you give your care giver a leave,
you are likely to be putting yourself and your family into a state of
high anxiety.

So why do it? If she's good, and your kids are attached to her, and
you trust her, you might want to have her back when she's straight-
ened out her problems. She might be a person you want to have
working for you for years to come, and if so, a month of inconve-
nience now may well be worth it to you in the long run.

If you decide that you can give your care giver a leave of absence,
and there is time to prepare (as for example, with maternity leave),
try to get her to help you find a suitable temporary replacement. If
she is truly responsible, she will help.

KEEPING IT LEGAL

Legally, you must pay taxes, but not everyone does. Some people
work off-the-books simply to avoid paying taxes. Others do it to

maintain eligibility for public assistance or unemployment insurance. Many employers find that having off-the-books workers is in their interest as well: It simplifies matters, eliminating the need to keep records, and it cuts costs, because employers are required to pay taxes, on top of wages, for legal employees.

If you choose to pay employment taxes, you are required by law to keep records of what you pay to whom and when. You are required to keep a record of (and to pay) several different kinds of tax, including Social Security and unemployment insurance. You can't pay one tax and not another.

When you figure out your own costs in employing a childcare worker, you'll be in for a rude surprise if you don't budget in the employment taxes that *you* must pay (there are some taxes *she* must pay). Whether you pay by cash or by check, weekly or biweekly, you've got to pay the taxman. It takes time and money, but it's the law.

PAYROLL TAXES

There are some employment agencies that pay childcare people their salary and medical benefits, as well as filing all the appropriate paperwork for taxes. Chances are, however, that you'll be dealing with the taxes yourself.

If you're paying payroll taxes, the first thing you should do is get a Federal Employer Identification Number (EIN) from the Internal Revenue Service (IRS) (Form SS-4). Subsequently, whenever you file returns or make payments, you will be identified by the EIN assigned to you.

It's also a good idea to get *The Employer's Tax Guide* from the IRS, as well as any equivalent publication put out by your state tax department. That way you'll be able to refer to good, official summaries of your tax liabilities and responsibilities whenever you need them.

Your employee must have a Social Security number. Household workers are exempt from income tax withholding (but not income tax); if you and your care giver both wish to deduct income tax, it is allowable. If she chooses to have her income tax withheld, she is also required to fill out either an IRS Form W-4 or the simpler Form W-4A, both of which help her compute her tax withholding allowance. You must file the following:

- Copies of Form W-2 Wage and Tax Statement (which summarizes pay and deductions) with both the IRS and your state tax office. You must also give your employee copies of this form by the end of January of each year to file with federal and state tax authorities. You must file a separate Form W-2 for each employee in February of each year for wages and taxes paid her the previous year. In addition, you must file a Form W-3, summarizing your annual payroll and taxes.

- Each January you must also file IRS Form 940 (Federal Unemployment Tax) and four times a year you must file IRS Form 942 (Employer's Quarterly Tax Return for Household Employees).

- You are also responsible for filing state unemployment insurance tax forms.

EARNED INCOME CREDIT (EIC)

Your childcare person may be eligible for an income tax refund if she does not have income tax withheld. Should she qualify, she can choose to receive advance EIC payments during the year rather than waiting to claim the EIC on her tax return. (Refer to IRS Form 942 for more information.)

SOCIAL SECURITY

Form 942 is used to compute and pay Social Security (FICA) taxes. These taxes are paid quarterly to the IRS, one month after the end of the pay period for which you are filing.

Social Security is a federal insurance program; it provides benefits to workers and their families in the event of disability, death, and retirement (at age sixty-two and over). They are payable for any employee who earns more than $50 in a quarter. (What this means, in effect, is that you are required to file even for employees who work only one day for you in a three-month period.)

Social Security taxes are currently 15.02 percent of the total cash wages. Half (7.51 percent) is to be paid by the employer and half by the employee. (That means if you're paying a gross salary of $200 a week, you owe $15.02 and withhold an additional $15.02 from her pay.) To simplify matters for the care giver, some household employers pay both parts of the employee's Social Security tax and pay a net wage. The employee's Form W-2 should thus show one-half of the Social Security paid as taxable income.

UNEMPLOYMENT INSURANCE

Form 940 is the Federal Unemployment Tax (FUTA) Return. It is filed in conjunction with state unemployment tax forms, and what you pay in state unemployment taxes is credited toward your federal payment. Unemployment insurance provides payments to unemployed (but employable) workers for a predetermined period or until they find a job. The payment (as well as the eligibility period) varies from state to state, but it is always capped and is generally half of weekly gross pay. If an employee quits or is fired for cause, she is not eligible to collect unemployment insurance; if however, you let someone go because your child is grown, or because you're moving, or for some other reason that is unrelated to her job performance, then she is eligible.

Employers are responsible for paying unemployment tax; it must not be deducted from employee's wages. You must pay federal unemployment tax if you paid cash wages of $1,000 or more in any calendar quarter in the current or preceding year. State requirements vary. For example, you must pay New York State unemployment tax if you pay cash wages of $500 or more to household workers in a calendar quarter.

The rate you are charged for unemployment insurance varies depending on what is called your "experience rating." The experience rating is computed based on your previous dealings with the unemployment insurance system. If you have no previous experience paying into the fund, or if your former employees have filed for benefits, you will have a higher rate. Conversely, your rate will be lower if your previous employees have not filed for benefits. You also receive a credit for paying into your state unemployment insurance fund. You cannot pay Social Security taxes and avoid paying unemployment insurance.

WORKERS' COMPENSATION AND DISABILITY

These are benefits that help protect workers from economic catastrophe. Workers' compensation is protection for job-related injuries or illness. Depending on the plan, compensation pays medical costs and sometimes provides pay for time lost from work.

Your homeowner's policy may include compensation coverage for household employees; if you have a homeowner's plan it makes sense to look over your policy or check with your agent about whether you're covered. Compensation plans are also available through some state insurance funds as well as through separate plans offered by private insurance carriers.

If you employ someone forty hours or more per week, compensation coverage is mandatory in New York state; it is not mandatory for part-time employees (who work fewer than forty hours). If you have a live-in worker, she is considered, for workers' compensation purposes, to have a twenty-four-hour day. (Check requirements with your state workers' compensation board.)

State disability coverage provides income replacement for workers who are physically unable to work. Eligibility depends completely on inability to work; it is not dependent on job-relatedness. In general, an employer is not required to carry disability insurance for workers if there is only one person working in the home. In New York State, for example, it is mandatory if an individual or company employs four or more people.

CHILDCARE TAX CREDIT ALLOWANCE

If either you or your spouse are working, seeking employment, are disabled, or a part-time student and you pay someone to care for your child, you may be eligible for a tax credit. There are a number of guidelines that determine eligibility. We suggest you refer to federal income tax Form 2441 for more information. If you intend to claim a tax credit and/or if you receive benefits from your employer's dependent-care assistance program, you must report your childcare person's name, address, and Social Security number.

MEDICAL BENEFITS

There are other benefits that are not required, but that you may wish to add to your care giver's total compensation package. Probably the most valuable (and certainly the most expensive) is medical insurance.

Thirty-seven million Americans have no health insurance, and 60 percent of all those who are uninsured are employed. Some "low-income" workers may be partially covered by Medicaid or Medicare. But many people have no medical benefits at all. It is, therefore, very likely that, even if your childcare worker is a legal, taxpaying employee, she and her family may have no coverage. So, if she is not covered under a spouse's or parent's plan, medical insurance may be the one extra benefit that is most useful to her.

Pediatrician Dr. Ramon Murphy spoke quite clearly with us about this issue. He made a very persuasive case that the one perk you should add for the person who takes care of your children is health-insurance coverage. He felt that medical benefits are a necessity for everyone and that it's a sign to your care giver that she, and the job she does, are important to you. Even if health insurance is offered in place of a bonus, Dr. Murphy felt that employers should take the responsibility of making sure their care givers are covered.

But it's not that easy, and it is expensive. You may try to get her on your group plan (this is easier if you own a business), or you may just help her find a plan to which you can contribute. You may consider carrying insurance from an organization of which you are a member (such as alumni or religious groups), many of which offer insurance plans for members. Two other groups that offer insurance plans are Association for Childhood Education International and National Association for the Education of Young Children (see appendix G for addresses). When providing coverage, you can work out a mutually acceptable arrangement: You might pay the entire cost, you may take deductions for health insurance out of her salary, or you may work out a combination, in which you are responsible for part of the cost while deducting the rest from her salary. Either way, you must get written permission from her in order to include her on a health-insurance plan.

OTHER BUSINESS DECISIONS

Some companies now offer "flexible benefit" plans. These plans allow employees to pick and choose the benefits they want. Under these plans, parents can authorize their employers to withhold a percentage of gross wages to cover childcare and other services not generally included in a regular benefits package. The withheld money is placed in a fund and can be used solely for the purpose designated. Employees benefit because their gross income is reduced by the dollar amount placed in the fund, thus resulting in a lower taxable income. Your company benefits department can tell you if this money-saving option is available to you.

If your care giver is expected to drive the family car, it's a good idea to include her as a driver in your auto insurance policy. This extra protection may be invaluable in case of an accident. (If she is to be a driver, we suggest that you ask to see her driver's license, ask if she took a driver's education course, inquire about speeding tickets and other violations, take a drive with her behind the wheel, and spell out the rules about guest passengers, seat belts, and car seats.)

It makes sense to discuss, and agree on, arrangements for telephone use, travel provisions (for au pairs and long-distance commuters), and live-in conditions with your childcare person.

It's also wise to make your financial arrangements clear from the start, and to explain what you're doing. Say, for example, that your care giver receives a net salary of $250 a week. In addition, you are paying her share, as well as your own, of Social Security. You are also taking responsibility for providing medical insurance and voluntary disability coverage. Your care giver's friends who work in the neighborhood are taking home $275, and she subsequently feels that she's underpaid. Sit down with her and explain the real value of her financial package. Let her know that the $250 she takes home is her *net*, and that her *actual gross* is closer to $300 a week. She'll be happier, and you will be too.

In the end, the business of taking care of your children is different from any other. It's a business based on trust and personal relationships. Its effectiveness cannot be quantified. Your care giver is not just cleaning your house, or putting together microchips. More than anything else, it's the quality of care that counts. And making it work requires more than just business sense; you need a little luck, a lot of thought, and sensitivity to the needs of your care giver, yourself, and most of all, your child.

Appendix A

NEWSPAPERS FOR CLASSIFIED AD PLACEMENT

Deseret News and Salt Lake Tribune
157 Regent Street
Salt Lake City, UT 84111
(801)237–2800

Irish Echo
309 Fifth Avenue
New York, NY 10016
(212)686–1266

New York Times
229 West 43rd Street
New York, NY 10036
(212)354–3900
(800)223–7437

Minneapolis Star and Tribune
425 Portland Avenue
Minneapolis, MN 55488
(612)372–4141

Milwaukee Journal
Milwaukee Sentinel
Box 661
333 West State Street
Milwaukee, WI 53201
(414)224–2000

Portland Press Herald
390 Congress Street
P.O. Box 1460
Portland, ME 04104
(207)775–5811

Grand Forks Herald
Box 6008
Grand Forks, ND 58206
(701)780–1100

International Herald Tribune
850 Third Avenue
New York, NY 10022
(212)752–3890

*Appendix B**

U.S. GOVERNMENT DESIGNATED AU PAIR PROGRAMS

Au Pair Homestay USA
Suite 1100
1411 K Street NW
Washington, DC 20005
(202)628–7134

EF Au Pair
EF Foundation
One Memorial Drive
Cambridge, MA 02142
(800)333–6056

Au Pair in America
American Institute for Foreign
  Study (AIFS)
102 Greenwich Avenue
Greenwich, CT 06830
(203)869–9090

eurAuPair
238 North Coast Highway
Laguna Beach, CA 92651
(800)333–3804

International Family Companion
(ten-week summer au pairs)
American Institute for Foreign
  Study
102 Greenwich Avenue
Greenwich, CT 06830
(203)869–9090

* This list and following pages do not constitute an endorsement by the author.

218

Appendix C

MEMBERS OF THE AMERICAN COUNCIL OF NANNY SCHOOLS

*† American Nanny Plan, Inc.
P.O. Box 790
Claremont, CA 91711
Beverly Benjamin, Ph.D.
(714)624–7711

† Bryan Nanny School
5000 Sumner Street
Lincoln, NB 68506
Debra Border
(402)483–3801

*† California Nanny College
2740 Fulton Avenue Suite 129
Sacramento, CA 95821
Larry Uno
(916)484–0163

*† C.A.P.E. Center, Inc.
(Childcare Alternative and
    Parent Education)
5924 Royal Lane, Suite 216
Dallas, TX 75230
Madeline Ehlert, M.Ed.
(214)692–0263

*† College of Mount St. Joseph
    on-the-Ohio
Child Care Professional Program
5701 Delhi Road
Mount St. Joseph, OH 45051
Ester Green-Merritt, Ed.D.
(513)244–4200

* ACNS charter member.
† Placement service.

Colorado Nanny Academy
Morgan Community College
17800 Road 20
Ft. Morgan, CO 80701
Corliss Keown
(303)867-3081

*† Delta College Nanny Training
   Program
University Center, MI 48710
Joy Shelton
(517)686-9417

DeMarge College, Inc.
DeMarge Employment Agency Inc.
3608 Northwest Fifty-eighth Street
Oklahoma City, OK 73112
Argie Caporal
(405)947-1534

*† English Nannies School
University Circle
11125 Magnolia Drive
Cleveland, OH 44106
Sheilagh Roth
(216)231-1515

Lovegrove School for Nannies
10 East Chase Street
Baltimore, MD 21202
Karen Lane
(301)234-0555

The Nanny Academy
Box 2173
Lakeland, FL 33803
Mickey Roberts, Ed.D.
(813)682-8749

† Nanny Academy of
   America, Inc.
171 Lakeshore Road
Grosse Pointe, MI 48236
Marguerite Michels, R.N.
(313)884-7550

*† Nanny Child Caring Plan, Inc.
511 Eleventh Avenue South
P.O. Box 95
Minneapolis, MN 55415
Jacqueline Richardson, Ph.D.
(612)375-0435

*† Nanny Institute of Beverly Hills
9470 Wilshire Boulevard
Beverly Hills, CA 90212
Sandra Lewis, R.N., M.N.
(213)278-8222
(800)446-8884

North American Nannies Institute
61 Jefferson Avenue
Columbus, OH 43215
Judith Bunge, Ph.D.
(614)228-6264

* ACNS charter member.
† Placement service.

Northern Virginia Community
 College
Early Childhood Education
3001 North Beauregard Street
Alexandria, VA 22311
Eula Miller
(703)845–6224

*† Northwest Nannies Institute
2100 Northeast Broadway, Suite 3F
Portland, OR 97232
Carolyn Kavanaugh
Linda Roffee
(503)284–1240

Oakton Community College
Nanny Certificate Program
1600 East Golf Road
Des Plaines, IL 60016
Florence Munuz
(312)635–1695

The Pennsylvania State University
College of Human Development
University Park, PA 16802
Theresa French
(814)865–1751

Reading Area Community College
P.O. Box 1706
Reading, PA 19603
Judith Peterson
(215)372–4721

St. Joseph Hospital School of
 Health Occupations
5 Woodward Avenue
Nashua, NH 03061
Camilie Twiss, R.N., M.S.
(603)882–3000

* Seattle Central Community
 College
Certified Nanny Program
1701 Broadway
Seattle, WA 98122
Gloria Myre
(206)587–6900

*† Sheffield School
Box 98, Route 518
Hopewell, NJ 08525
Ellyn Sheffield
(609)737–8813

Tidewater Community College
State Route 135
Portsmouth Campus
Portsmouth, VA 23703
Ramona Rapp
(804)484–2121

* ACNS charter member.
† Placement service.

Appendix D

MEMBERS OF THE INTERNATIONAL NANNY ASSOCIATION

United States (Alphabetical by State and City)

* Care by Nannys
405 Second Avenue SW
Cullman, AL 35055
Carol Adams, president
(205)739–2939

* Professional Rent A Mom
7926 Old Seward Highway
No. C-8
Anchorage, AK 99518
Rhoda Turinsky, owner
(907)349–4463
(907)349–6391

† Glendale Community College
6000 West Olive
Glendale, AZ 85302
Eileen Shiff, program director
(602)435–3196

* Attention Unlimited
3310 West Bell Road, #19
Phoenix, AZ 85023
Kathy Price-Lawler, president
(602)978–2306

† Quapaw Community Y Nanny
500 Quapaw Avenue
Hot Springs, AR 71901
Sandi Jordan, director, nanny
  institute
(501)623–9922
(501)624–0774

† Chaffey Community College
5885 Haven Avenue
Alta Loma, CA 91705
Deborah Davis
(714)987–1737

* Placement agency.
† Public training program.

222

* Baby Buddy, Inc.
226 West Beverly Drive
Beverly Hills, CA 90212
Cathy Orell
(213)273–2330
(213)454–5413

† Nanny Institute of Beverly Hills
9470 Wilshire Boulevard
Beverly Hills, CA 90212
Sandra Lewis, president
(213)278–8222
(800)446–8884

‡ Grossmont College
8800 Grossmont College Drive
El Cajon, CA 92020
Catherine Robertson, nanny
    instructor/coordinator
(619)465–1700, x280
(619)443–6557

† Newport Nanny College
18582 Beach Boulevard, Suite 222
Huntington Beach, CA 92648
Suzanne Butnik, co-director/owner
(714)968–0380
(714)854–0491

* Mothers-In-Deed
425 Sherman Avenue, Suite 130
Palo Alto, CA 94306
Dale Mnookin
(415)326–8570

‡ Diablo Valley College/Family Life
321 Golf Club Road
Pleasant Hill, CA 94523
Norma J. Meyerholz, instructor,
    ECE
(415)685–1230, x3316
(415)834–0991

* E & R Nanny Agency, Inc.
7311 Greenhaven Drive, Suite 100A
Sacramento, CA 95831
B. Kay Ericson, president
(916)424–8579
(916)428–2391

* Naturally Nannys Agency
4926 La Cuenta, Suite 203-C
San Diego, CA 92124
Janice Campbell, owner
(691)268–8030
(691)292–1616

‡ San Diego Mesa College
7250 Mesa College Drive
San Diego, CA 92111
Sally Pike
(619)560–2649

* Be In Our Care Agency
31 La Mesa Lane
Walnut Creek, CA 94598
Bea Littlejohn, director/owner
(415)933–2273
(415)939–5695

---

* Placement agency.
† Private school with placement service.
‡ Public training program.

* Children's Services/City of
   Boulder
P.O. Box 791
Boulder, CO 80306
Kathleen Shindler, coordinator
(303)441–3180
(303)449–7133

* Nanny Poppins
1931 East Kentucky Avenue
Denver, CO 80209
Karen Jackson, president
(303)722–7778

* Starkey and Associates, Inc.
360 South Monroe Street, Suite 220
Denver, CO 80209
Mary Starkey, president
(303)394–4904

* Colorado Nanny Academy/
   Morgan
17800 Road 20
Fort Morgan, CO 80701
Karen Michie, director
(303)867–3081

* Help Mates Unlimited
3 Terrace Drive
Bethel, CT 06801
Celeste A. Tutko, president
(800) LIVE–INS
(203)792–4798

* The Fairfield Au Pair Agency, Inc.
18 Chestnut Street
Cos Cob, CT 06807
Denise M. Williams, president
(203)869–8682
(203)629–2636

* Nannie Network, Inc.
P.O. Box 2423
Darien, CT 06820
Carolyne E. McEnery, president
(203)358–9800
(800) 87–NANNY

* Au Pair in America (AIFS)
102 Greenwich Avenue
Greenwich, CT 06830
Lauren Kratovil, director
(203)863–6130

* Nannies Unlimited
83 Boston Post Road
Guilford, CT 06437
Linda A. Rosenbaum,
   president/owner
(203)453–6664

* Need-A-Nanny Agency
9 Karen Drive
New Fairfield, CT 96812
Dana Redding Welles,
   director/owner
(203)746–7217

* Placement agency.

* TGIF USA
P.O. Box 828
Old Lyme, CT 06371
Joanne Kobar, president and
    national franchisor
(203)434–1262

* Classic Care
6 Landmark Square
Stamford, CT 06901
Nina A. Schmidt, director
(203)329–9055
(203)329–9625

* Overseas Custom—Maid Agency
300 Bedford Street
Stamford, CT 06901
Alan Wildstein, owner
(203)324–9575
(203)531–8579

* HELP!
15 Bridge Road
Weston, CT 06883
Doris Elliott, president
(203)226–3456
(203)226–4209

* Helping Hands, Inc.
P.O. Box 7068
Wilton, CT 06897
Sharlene Martin, president
(203)834–1742
(203)834–1332

* In Home Care
608 East Altamonte Drive, Suite 206
Altamonte Springs, FL 32701
J. D. Spenser
(407)260–9611

* Nannies Etc., Inc.
2400 East Las Olas Boulevard
Suite E
Ft. Lauderdale, FL 33301
Dorothy L. Mars, president
(305)527–4935

* The Nanny Network, Inc.
20145 Northeast Twenty-fifth
    Avenue
Miami, FL 33269
Roni K. Fertig, president
(305)932–5335

* Bib's Family Tyes, Inc.
420 US Highway #1, Suite 211
North Palm Beach, FL 33408
Bryna Jagoda, president
(407)775–1687
(407)626–7257

† Sarasota Vocational Center
4748 Beneva Road
Sarasota, FL 34233
Joyce Brown, assistant director,
    home economics
(813)924–1365

* Placement agency.
† Public training program.

* Nannies For Hire, Inc.
15932 West State Road 84
Sunrise, FL 33326
Joy Reisner, president
(305)389–5766
(305)384–6384

* Home Care Alternatives
3225 South MacDill Avenue
Suite 133–210
Tampa, FL 33629
Terry R. Watson, president
(813)785–3544
(813)254–1396

* Friend of the Family
895 Mt. Vernon Highway
Atlanta, GA 30327
Judi Merlin, president
(404)255–2848
(404)256–9218

* The Sitters of Atlanta, Inc.
1246 Concord Road, Suite 201
Smyrna, GA 30080
Heidi A. Anderson, director
(404)435–6250
(404)433–9932

* Hawaii Nanny Service, Inc.
365-H Haleloa Place
Honolulu, HI 96821
Nicolette Davis, president
(808)533–7756

† Honolulu Community College
874 Dillingham Boulevard
Honolulu, HI 96817
Miles P. Nakanishi,
    instructor, human services
(808)845–9259
(808)456–2180

* Nanny Network of Hawaii
46–001 Kam Highway, Suite 322
Kaneohe, HI 96744
Beatrice Hawkins, owner
(808)247–8145

† Oakton Community College
1600 East Golf Road
Des Plaines, IL 60016
Florence Munuz
(312)635–1695

* NannySitters, Inc.
2500 West Higgins Road
Hoffman Estates, IL 60195
Dorene Sidbeck, manager/owner
(312)885–1700
(312)837–2433

* Jewish Day Care, Inc.
910 Polk Boulevard
Des Moines, IA 50312
Suzanne J. McKinley,
    program director
(515)223–9547
(515)277–6321

* Placement agency.
† Public training program.

* Nannies of Kansas City, Ltd.
9318 Roe Avenue
Prairie Village, KS 66207
Sharon Hites, president/owner
(913)341–6447

† Cloud County Community
College
2221 Campus Drive
P.O. Box 1002
Concordia, KS 66901
Joan Raven Robinson,
childcare coordinator
(913)243–1435

‡ Markham School for Nannies
14700 West Kellogg
Wichita, KS 67235
Tina and Annette Markham,
executive directors
(316)722–5660
(316)794–2966

† Sullivan Junior College of
Business
P.O. Box 33–308
Louisville, KY 40232
Merry Q. Denny, coordinator
(502)451–0841
(502)454–4878

* Portland Nannies
106 Park Street Row
Portland, ME 04101
June Fitzpatrick, director
(207)77–CHILD
(207)773–6574

* The Perfect Nanny Ltd.
3 Church Circle, Suite 175
Annapolis, MD 21401
Laura Deane, director
(301)974–8090
(301)268–3573

‡ A Choice Nanny
8950 Route 108, Gorman Plaza
Columbia, MD 21045
Jacqueline Clark, president
(301)730–2229

* Helping Hands, Inc.
8008 Phirne Road East
Glen Burnie, MD 21061
Maureen Radtke,
recruitment counselor
(301)969–2846
(301)969–7412

* American Au Pair, Inc.
P.O. Box 97, New Town Branch
Boston, MA 02258
Marsha Epstein, president
(617)244–5154
(617)969–5121

* Placement agency.
† Public training program.
‡ Private school with placement service.

* Beacon Hill Nannies, Inc.
121 Mt. Vernon Street
Boston, MA 02108
Paula Chiungos, owner
(617)227–5592

* The Nurturing Nanny, Inc.
346 Beacon Street
Boston, MA 02116
Wendi Harrison McKenna,
  director
(617)424–6757

* N.E. Nanny Connection Inc.
11 Anderson Drive
Boxford, MA 01921
Patricia C. Duffey, president
(508)352–7653

* Child Care Placement
Service, Inc.
149 Buckminster Road
Brookline, MA 02146
Allene Fisch, owner/director
(617)566–6294
(617)277–5620

* Quality Nannies, Inc.
44 Brentwood Road
Chelmsford, MA 01824
Mary Lee Hatch,
  managing director
(508)250–1712
(508)256–4059

* In Search of Nanny, Inc.
Liberty Square, Suite 115
Danvers, MA 01923
Betty Davis, director
(617)777–9891

† New England School for
  Nannies, Inc.
41 Baymor Drive
East Longmeadow, MA 01028
Karen Hamlin, president
(413)525–1861
(413)525–2546

* Family Focus, Inc.
P.O. Box 8093
One Apple Hill, Route 9
Natick, MA 01760
Jane Arcese, president
(508)877–5575

* Knights Bridge Associates
251 West Central Street, Suite 141
Natick, MA 01760
Diane Swartz, N.N.E.B.,
  consultant
(508)881–8070
(508)881–8252

† Professional Nanny, Inc.
354 Washington Street
Wellesley, MA 02181
Anne Merchant, president
(617)237–0211
(617)655–0313

* Placement agency.
† Private school with placement service.

* Nanny Service
26 Haviland Street
Worcester, MA 01602
Judy Shapiro, director
(508)755–9284

† Alpena Senior High School
3303 Third Avenue
Alpena, MI 49707
Ron Lemke, vocational placement
  director
(517)356–6161, x276
(517)356–3077

* The Nanny Corporation
315 East Eisenhower Parkway
Suite 300
Ann Arbor, MI 48108
Katheryn A. Shick, president
(313)973–CARE
(313)971–8272

‡ The Nanny Network, Inc.—
  Wattles
Executive Suites North
2161 Seventeen Mile Road
Sterling Heights, MI 48310
Linda Hice-Guastella, president
(313)939–KIDS

* Granny's Nannies
P.O. Box 146
Brainerd, MN 56401
Doris L. Ulrich, owner
(218)828–4289

* Nanny Solutions, Inc.
4244 Alden Drive
Edina, MN 55416
Kimberly Collins Parizeau, partner
(612)922–5141

* National Nanny Resource and
  Referral
3300 County Road 10, #410
Minneapolis, MN 55429
Bonnie Roeder, director
(612)566–1561

† University of Minnesota—
  Crookston
Hospitality and Home Economics
  Division
Minneapolis, MN 56716
Glenn Olsen, Ph.D.,
  division chairperson
(218)281–6510
(218)281–2062

* Placement agency.
† Public training program.
‡ Private school with placement service.

* Red Wing Technical Institute
Highway 58
Red Wing, MN 55066
Nancy B. Swanson, administrative
  assistant
(612)388–8271
(612)388–8622

† CSI Nanny Professionals
245 East Sixth Street, Suite 703
St. Paul, MN 55101
Dr. Jean Hanson, president
(612)221–0587
(612)483–9261

‡ Technical Education Center
245 East Sixth Street, Suite 703
St. Paul, MN 55101
Dr. Jean Hanson, director
(612)221–0587
(612)483–9261

† Heartland Nannies
210 North Higgins Avenue
Suite 306
P.O. Box 9237
Missoula, MT 59802
Karen Ryan, owner
(406)542–0241
(406)721–9246
(406)542–6673

† TLC, Inc.
7301 Tulane
St. Louis, MO 63130
Sharon Graff, president
(314)725–5660

† Gingerbread Nanny
305 East Walnut
Springfield, MO 65802
Frances Banes Crighton,
  secretary/treasurer
(417)886–2669
(417)869–4943

* Central Community College
Box 1024
Hastings, NE 68901
Marilyn Gerritson
(308)384–5220

§ Bryan Memorial Hospital
5000 Sumner Street
Lincoln, NE 68506
Debra Border, coordinator
(402)483–3801
(402)421–1786

† Helping Hands, Inc.
1109 West Avon Lane
Lincoln, NE 68505
Terri Mecham Butler,
  recruitment counselor
(402)467–3192

* Public training program.
† Placement agency.
‡ Private training program.
§ Private school with placement service.

* Southeast Community College
8800 O Street
Lincoln, NE 68520
Alicia Baillie,
    program supervisor—
    child development services
(402)471-3333
(402)423-9212

* McCook Community College
1205 East Third Street
McCook, NE 69001
Jerda Garcy
(308)345-6303

† The Nanny Company
3214 North Ninety-seventh
    Street, #192
Omaha, NE 68134
Billie J. Bastian, owner
(402)573-1254

‡ Omaha Child Care Referral
5015 Dodge Street, #2
Omaha, NE 68132
Christie Bower, director of
    resource and referral
(402)551-2379

† The Nanny Solution, Inc.
P.O. Box 278
Bedford, NH 03102
Sheryl Hammond, owner
(603)472-2719

† Nanny Care
365 Newman Avenue
Seecook, NH 02771
Kathleen Swift
(401)847-8000
(617)336-4352

† Caregivers
6–12 North Union Avenue
Cranford, NJ 07016
Pat Barnett, director
(201)272-3180

§ American Nanny Academy, Inc.
7 Utica Road
Edison, NJ 08820
Maureen Simko Hreha, R.N.,
    M.S.N., director
(201)906-6354
(201)494-2457

† Help Finders Unlimited, Inc.
16 West Palisade Avenue
Englewood, NJ 07631
Diana Wright, president
(201)871-4414
(201)872-1583

† American Nanny Placement
    Association
219 North Martine Avenue
Fanwood, NJ 07203
Margaret Larosa, owner/director
(201)322-5252

* Public training program.
† Placement agency.
‡ Private school with placement service.
§ Private training program.

* Kare for Kids Inc.
101 Prospect Avenue
Hackensack, NJ 07601
Sharn Floch, president/owner
(201)666–9539
(201)666–1888

† Neighborhood Nannies, Inc.
203 Kings Highway East
Haddonfield, NJ 08033
Sandra Costantino,
  executive director
(609)795–5833
(609)428–9522

* Nannies Plus
615 West Mt. Pleasant Avenue
Livingston, NJ 07039
Joy Wayne, director
(201)992–5800

* Nannies, USA, Inc.
P.O. Box 7432
Princeton, NJ 08543
Mimi Hafeman, owner
(609)799–4556
(609)799–2447

* Nanny Placement, Inc.
4 Schuh Road
Princeton, NJ 08540
Katherine Hofmann,
  placement coordinator
(609)737–8211
(609)924–7151

* Princeton Nanny Placement
301 North Harrison Street
Suite 416
Princeton, NJ 08540
Marjorie A. Biddle, Ph.D., director
(609)497–1195
(609)497–1193

Good Help, Inc.
P.O. Box 627
Sparta, NJ 07871
Deborah Drumm, president
(201)729–HELP
(201)729–8034

* At Your Service
120 County Road
Tenafly, NJ 07670
Sue Breckwold, owner
(201)894–5339
(201)567–2884

* Child Care Decisions
80 Business Park Drive
Armonk, NY 10521
Daryl Dunlavy, president
(914)747–1445

* National Nanny Placement
  Service
38 Main Street
Chatham, NY 12037
Deborah J. Schwarz, president
(518)392–4498

* Placement agency.
† Private school with placement service.

* The Nanny's Place, Inc.
500 Chestnut Ridge Road
Chestnut Ridge, NY 10977
Valerie Klein, president
(914)425–7268
(914)425–4770

* Nannies of Suffolk, Inc.
27 Black Locust Avenue
East Setauket, NY 11733
JoAnn Gross Cohn, owner
(516)331–9875

* Goodhelper Domestic Agency
33–70 Prince Street, Suite 208
Flushing, NY 11354
Mei Ling Moe, owner
(718)463–0300
(718)224–9534

* Nannies For You, Inc.
12 A Chatsworth Avenue, #355
Larchmont, NY 10538
Leslie Sullivan, director
(914)834–4408
(914)833–1175

† Sullivan County Community
    College
Early Childhood, Nursery
    Education Program
Loch Sheldrake, NY 12759
Mary A. Wilson, director, ECE/
    nursery education programs
(914)434–5750, x305

* Lynn Agency, Inc.
2067 Broadway, Suite 68
New York, NY 10023
Marcia Trupin, president/owner
(212)874–6130

* Professional Nannies
    Institute, Inc.
501 Fifth Avenue
New York, NY 10017
Denyse Kapelus, director
(212)692–9510

‡ VIP, Inc.
69 Monroe Avenue, Suite A
Pittsford, NY 14534
Linda Underhill,
    director nanny training
(716)385–9850
(716)461–4880

* American Nanny Network Inc.
63 Brown Avenue
Rye, NY 10580
Kathleen C. Haire, president
(914)921–0636
(914)967–2213

* Custom Childcare Services
30 West Nyack Village Square
West Nyack, NY 10994
Dr. Lynne Schwartz, director
(914)638–2085

* Placement agency.
† Public training program.
‡ Private school with placement service.

* Security Blanket Child Care
   Service
P.O. Box 1882
Williamsville, NY 14221
Sarah Sawyer, director
(716)878–2339

* American Nannies of
   Charlotte, Inc.
4139 Rutherford Drive
Charlotte, NC 28210
Karen W. Percival, president
(704)552–7757

* Kid Care Connections, Inc.
2614 Roswell Avenue
Charlotte, NC 28209
Judy F. Shelley, president
(704)372–3655
(704)541–3560

* The Nanny Network
P.O. Box 2011
Charlotte, NC 28247
Cynthia Bergren, president
(704)543–4610

* Nannies & Grannies
7 Battleground Court
Greensboro, NC 27408
Susan E. Rivenbark, president
(919)379–0527
(919)294–1816

* Nanny's Here, Ltd.
3500 Vest Mill Road, Suite 24
Winston-Salem, NC 27103
Leatha P. Ritchie, president
(919)760–9010
(919)766–0826

† English Nannies School
11125 Magnolia Drive
Cleveland, OH 44106
Sheilagh G. Roth,
   executive director
(216)231–1515
(216)463–2238

† North American Nannies
   Institute
61 Jefferson Avenue
Columbus, OH 43215
Judith A. Bunge,
   executive director
(614)228–6264
(614)481–8205

* Child Care Insights, Inc.
14701 Detroit Avenue, Suite 505
Lakewood, OH 44107
Elisabeth A. Bryenton, owner
(216)221–3300

† Nannies of Cleveland, Inc.
15707 Detroit Avenue
Lakewood, OH 44107
Monica Bassett, R.N., president
(216)521–4650
(216)228–5743

* Placement agency.
† Private school with placement service.

* DeMarge College, Inc.
see p. 220 (appendix C)

† Nannies, Etc.
2817 Quail Plaza Drive
Oklahoma City, OK 73120
Michelle Hafner, president
(405)751–4180
(405)433–2123

‡ Tulsa County A.V.T. School
3802 North Peoria
Tulsa, OK 74145
Karen Weiss, coordinator
(918)428–2261
(918)742–1433

† Regency Nanny Services
370 Lithia Way
Ashland, OR 97520
Roxanne Jones, president
(503)482–5716

† Child Care Solutions, Inc.
1455 Acacia
Eugene, OR 97401
Linda Riepe, president/owner
(503)687–1514
(503)687–1514

† Northwest Nannies, Inc.
2100 Northeast Broadway
Suite 3-F
Portland, OR 97232
Linda Roffe, president
(503)284–1240

† Rent-A-Mom of Oregon
5331 Southwest Macadam Street
Suite 282
Portland, OR 97201
Pam Israel, co-owner
(503)222–5779

† Moore's Nanny Agency
P.O. Box 815
Roseburg, OR 97470
Cherie Moore
(503)673–0064

† The Philadelphia Nanny Network
1528 Walnut Street, Suite 1626
Philadelphia, PA 19102
Wendy Sacks
(215)546–3002

§ Community College of Allegheny
1130 Perry Highway
Pittsburgh, PA 15237
Cyndi L. Syskowski, coordinator/
   professional nanny program
(412)734–4025
(412)441–1038

† Kids Care Express, Inc.
54 Fox Point Drive
Pittsburgh, PA 15238
Phyllis Majerick, president
(412)963–6647

* Private school with placement service.
† Placement agency.
‡ Educator.
§ Public training program.

* Rent-A-Mom, Inc.
503 B McKnight Park Drive
Pittsburgh, PA 15237
Dorothy Robison, president
(412)369–9113

* Nanny Solutions, Inc.
504 Heather Circle
Villanova, PA 19085
Linda Foster Whitton, partner
(215)971–1590

* A Choice Nanny of Yardley
Heston Hall, Suite 108
1790 Yardley-Langhorne Road
Yardley, PA 19027
Patricia B. Cardona, president
(215)493–9020
(215)493–9095

* New England Nanny Referrals
P.O. Box 8378
Cranston, RI 02910
Dorothy Caren,
   placement consultant
(401)943–4235

† National Nanny Brokers
P.O. Box 26
Narragansett, RI 02882
Elaine Mullen Cassinelli,
   owner/broker
(401)782–8762

* TLC For Kids, Inc.
P.O. Box 50637
Nashville, TN 37205
Michele Paul Bloemer, director
(615)646–8251

‡ The C.A.P.E. Center, Inc.
5924 Royal Lane, Suite 216
Dallas, TX 75230
Mary Jo Crist, vice-president
(214)692–0263
(214)231–5505

§ Houston Community College
3821 Caroline Street
Houston, TX 77004
Joan Wyde, Ph.D., department
   head child development
(713)630–1103
(713)721–2090

* Nannies and More, Inc.
700 Harwood Road, Suite G
Hurst, TX 76054
Susie Herren, president/owner
(817)478–7808
(817)572–3969

* La Petite Mere—Nanny Referral
P.O. Box 17041
Salt Lake City, UT 84117
Mike Bray, owner
(801)943–7788

* Placement agency.
† Placement agency and nanny broker.
‡ Private school with placement agency.
§ Public training program.

* The Vermont School for Nannies
207–217 Skitchewaug Trail
Springfield, VT 05156
Floreen Bishop
(802)885–3835

† Nanny Dimensions, Inc.
10875 Main Street, Suite 111
Fairfax, VA 22030
Gail C. Lyon, president
(703)273–3685
(703)352–4443

† Mom and Tot Nanny Agency
915 Lawton Street
McLean, VA 22101
Robin Crawford, owner
(703)827–0067
(703)847–8595

† Nanny Systems, Inc. (NSI)
1310 Monterey Avenue
Norfolk, VA 23508
Carey Keefe, president
(804)440–5410

† Real Care Connection, Inc.
1907 Hugenot Road, Suite 101
Richmond, VA 23235
Daphne Atherton, president
(804)379–9314
(804)794–4945
(804)794–0892

† New World Nannies
8706 Melwood Lane
Richmond, VA 23233
Lavinia Anne Recchia,
   vice-president
(804)282–6128
(804)740–6874

† The Nanny Factor, Inc.
P.O. Box 8188
Springfield, VA 22151
Leslie S. Smith, owner/president
(703)764–9021
(800) 232–NANY

† Rent-A-Mom
10202 Northeast One hundred
   ninety-seventh Street
Bothell, WA 98011
Dianne Heath-Parrott, owner
(206)624–2640

† Nanny USA, Inc.
8103 Bayridge Avenue
Gig Harbor, WA 98355
Marilyn Hoppen, president
(206)851–9678

† Nannybroker, Inc.
26520 Southeast One hundred
   fifty-seventh Street
Issaquah, WA 98027
Judi Julin, R.N., director/owner
(206)624–1213
(206)392–5681

* Private school with placement service.
† Placement agency.

* Mother Goose Nannys, Inc.
2335 Forty-seventh Avenue SW
Seattle, WA 98116
Trish Hughes, president
(206)932–0314

Helping Hands, Inc.
P.O. Box 9542
Spokane, WA 99204
Shirlee Burrage, director
(509)455–5409
(509)455–8054

* Nannyworks, Inc.
1859 Northeast One hundred
   fifty-fifth Street
Woodinville, WA 98072
Joan B. Pedersen, president
(206)788–4824
(206)788–4028

* Kidpanions, Inc.
Potomac Nannies
P.O. Box 6259
Washington, DC 20015
Diane Cross, co-director
(301)986–0048
(301)656–2089

* Mother's Helper Agency
1101 Fourteenth Street NW
Suite 1203
Washington, DC 20005
Marla Sanders, president
(202)842–3333

* Nanny Placement Services, Inc.
1621 Wisconsin Avenue NW
Washington, DC 20007
Courtney Hagner, president
(202)342–1405
(800) 34–NANNY

† Chippewa Valley Technical
   College
620 West Clairemont Avenue
Eau Claire, WI 54701
Renée Ramsay
(715)833–6237

† Moraine Park Technical College
235 North National Avenue
Fond du Lac, WI 54936
Barbara Lukas, nanny instructor
(414)922–8611
(414)923–0238

† Northeast Wisconsin Technical
1183 Circle Drive
Green Bay, WI 54313
Elizabeth Kaster, child care
   coordinator and lab school
   director
(414)498–5651
(414)494–4121

* Nannies For Hire, Inc.
6033 Monona Drive, Suite 100A
Madison, WI 53716
Ann Anderson, president
(608)221–8200

* Placement agency.
† Public training program.

* Gateway Technical College
1101 Main Street
Racine, WI 53403
G. Kragness
(414)631–7300

Foreign (Alphabetical by Country and City)

† Pam Arnold Center
25 Gresham Street
Adelaide, South Australia 5000
Australia
Pam Arnold, proprietor
08–231–2502

† Krisala Nannies/Australian
  Nanny
P.O. Box 4
Hawksburn, Victoria 3142
Australia
Kris Saldukas
03–515391
03–519335
052–788863

† Dial-a-Nanny
15th Floor Westpac Centre
109 St. George's Terrace
Perth, West Australia 6000
Australia
C.C. Rowley
09–321–7485

‡ Scotia Personnel Ltd.
P.O. Box 817
Amherst, N.S. B4H 4B9
Canada
M. A. "Marilyn" Von Snick,
  president
(902)667–7724

‡ U.K. Nannies
202-1501 Seventeenth Avenue SW
Calgary, Alta. T2T 0E2
Canada
Gillian Vass, owner
(403)244–2939
(403)244–7121

‡ Kingview Personnel
Box 1131
King City, Ont. LOG 1K0
Canada
Patricia Henry, director/owner
(416)727–1218
(416)841–1323

‡ European Nannies
101 Thorncliffe Park Drive
Toronto, Ont. M4H 1M2
Canada
Caroline Tapp-McDougall
(416)421–0596

* Public training program.
† Private school with placement service.
‡ Placement agency.

* Quality Care—The Complete
  Child
A-17, 445 Southwest Marine Drive
Vancouver, B.C. V5X 2R9
Canada
Ms. Lynne Johnson, owner
(604)325–7585

* Victoria Nanny Agency Ltd.
733 Johnson Street, Suite 214
Victoria, B.C. V8W 1M8
Canada
Joan Topham, president
(604)384–1220

* Help at Hand Nanny Agency
700 Great Cambridge Road
Eafield EN1 3RU
England
June Warriner, S.R.W.
01–364–0484
01–504–7193

* Regency Nannies
50 Hans Crescent
Knightsbridge, London SW1
England
Eileen Wright, principal
01–950–5084
01–225–1055

* Albermarle Nannies
45 Conduit Street
London W1R 9FB
England
Sheila Davis, managing director
01–493–2441
01–722–7502

* The Nanny Service
9 Paddington Street
London W1M 3CA
England
Paul Rendel, director
01–935–3515

† Princess Christian College
26 Wilbraham Road
Fallowfield, Manchester M14 6JX
England
Mary E. McRae, principal, nursery
  training
061–224–4560

† Chiltern Nursery Training
  College
16 Peppard Road
Caversham
Reading, Berkshire RG4 872
England
Pamela A. Townsend, principal
01–0734–471847

* Placement agency.
† Private training program.

* Jafe Poppins Service
Hasebe No. II Building IF 5–21–2
  Hiroo
Shibuya-ku, Tokyo
Japan
Noriko Nakamura, president
03–447–2100
03–442–1444

† Rangi Ruru Nanny School
59 Hewitts Road
Christchurch, 1
New Zealand
Jill Marie Bromley, director
03–556099
03–558702

* The Nanny Agency
P.O. Box 33–485
Hurstmerg Road
Takapuna, Auckland 9
New Zealand
Anne-Marie Bluemel, director
09–496–608

* Placement agency.
† Private training program.

Appendix E

POSTPARTUM CARE SERVICES

Aunties
P.O. Box 68
Sicklerville, NJ 08081
Shirley Himeback
Ruth Wilf
Connie Petrillo
(609)728–6430

The Fourth Trimester
4516 Holsten Hills Road
Knoxville, TN 37914
Beatrice Vogel
(615)522–2229

Maternal Instincts Ltd.
RD #2, Box 133K
Monroe, NY 10950
Dawn Salker
(914)496–7186

The Mom Service
78 Elm Road
Briarcliff Manor, NY 10510
Jane Arnold
(914)762–8243

M.O.M.S.
121 Summit Avenue
St. Louis, MO 63119
Gretchen Tickeral
Mary Magill
(314)962–7166

Mother Nurture
246–12 Sixtieth Avenue
Douglaston, NY 13362
Alice Gilgoff
(718)631–2229

MotherCare Services, Inc.
824 Massachusetts Avenue
Lexington, MA 02173
Joan Singer
(617)863–1333

Mothering Services of Portland
192 Stevens Avenue
Portland, ME 04101
Dory Richards
(207)774–8210

MotherLove
20 Ash Street
Westwood, NJ 07675
Debra Pascali
(201)358–2703

Motherlove
4414 Buxton Court
Indianapolis, IN 46254
Diane McQuiston
(317)293–7763

Mothertime
140 Christie Street
Leonia, NJ 07605
Charlotte Henshaw
(201)585–0846

Mothertime (Montclair)
13 Bellaire Drive
Montclair, NJ 07042
Melanie Smith
Diane Hogan
(201)744–3409

Mothertime (Teaneck)
1089 Queen Anne Road
Teaneck, NJ 07666
Melanie Smith
Kathie Colando
(201) 833–2259

Mothertime (Westfield)
500 Boulevard
Westfield, NJ 07090
Ellen Shurak
(201)654–1647

Mother's Helper
3326 Cambridge
St. Louis, MO 63143
Maureen Berra
(314)644–6241

Appendix F

ENGLISH NURSERY TRAINING COLLEGES

Chiltern Nursery Training College
16 Peppard Road
Caversham
Reading, Berkshire RG4 8JZ
England

Norland Nursery Training College
Denford Park
Hungerford, Berkshire RG17 0PQ
England

The Princess Christian College
26 Wilbraham Road
Fallowfield, Manchester M14 6JX
England

Appendix G

HEALTH INSURANCE AND OTHER INFORMATION

Related Organizations with Health-Insurance Plans

Association for Childhood Education International
11141 Georgia Avenue, Suite 200
Wheaton, MD 20902
(301)942–2443

National Association for the Education of Young Children
1834 Connecticut Avenue NW
Washington, DC 20009
(202)232–8777

Other Sources of Information

The National Nanny Newsletter
490 East Jefferson Avenue
Pomona, CA 91767
Deborah Davis, editor
(714)623–2635

245

Index

RUTH S. ELLIOTT has worked in the communications industry as an editor, reporter, and marketing and sales executive. She has worked for ABC, CBS, and Ziff-Davis. She is active in numerous industry and civic organizations and has served for five years on the board of directors of Advertising Women of New York. She has both a BA and an MBA degree. Most important, she is the mother of Kate and Maggie.

JIM SAVAGE is an advertising copywriter whose clients include some of America's largest direct marketers. He has also contributed to books, magazines, and works for musical theater.

362.7
E

22,009

Elliott, Ruth S.

Minding the kids: